DOWN TO EARTH

H.R.H. Prince Philip is President of the World Wildlife Fund International, now renamed the World Wide Fund For Nature. *Down to Earth* is a collection of his speeches and writings on the relationship of man with his environment from 1961 to 1987.

DOWN TO EARTH

Speeches and writings of

HIS ROYAL HIGHNESS
PRINCE PHILIP
DUKE OF EDINBURGH

*on the relationship of man
with his environment*

FONTANA/Collins

First published in Great Britain by
William Collins Sons & Co. Ltd 1988
First issued in Fontana Paperbacks 1989

Printed and bound in Great Britain by
William Collins Sons & Co. Ltd, Glasgow

CONTENTS

FOREWORD

Professor Mohammed Kassas

Nature conservation is a world movement. It aims to retain a balance in the processes of the biosphere and to instil quality in the human environment. It has now become an integral part of our culture. This is due, on the one hand, to the concern of national and international institutions to correct the assaults of excessive exploitation of natural resources and, on the other, to leaders who stand high as banners that map its road and direction.

During the last 25 years, His Royal Highness The Duke of Edinburgh has been prominent among such leaders and has actively helped the development of the basic principles of conservation and the dissemination of its message. The present volume contains a selection of his discourses on conservation. It shows that His Royal Highness has influenced the maturation of the guiding premises of conservation – from the early notion of the protection of species through to the modern perception of the necessity for the conservation of ecological elements and the broader concept of sustained development.

The reader will note that the first section (preface and part one) depicts this evolution; the second section (parts two and three) expounds the basics of conservation of the entire biosphere – maintenance of its quality and the sustenance of a benign relationship between population and the earth's productive capacity. The reader will also note a cord of ethical principles that runs through the whole book and which is distilled in the concluding section, 'The Moral Imperative'. These principles relate to our responsibilities towards future generations, our partner societies and our associate organisms, who are all shareholders of our grand ark.

This book provides glimpses of the notable contributions of His Royal Highness to the world conservation movement.

W. Kanas

Faculty of Science, University of Cairo

PREFACE

H.R.H. Prince Philip, Duke of Edinburgh

Any observant person living in a familiar countryside is certain to notice differences in the natural world about them between one year and another. Every year some plants and animals do better than others. There is a natural fluctuation in the breeding success of all wild species and the seasonal variation in climate affects trees and plants in different ways. It is this sort of awareness that rings the alarm bells when certain tree species develop a disease, or when there is continuing decline in the number of otters on a familiar stretch of river, or when there appear to be altogether too many corpses of small birds, as occurred when the organo-chlorine pesticides were first introduced. These things are unlikely to be noticed by laboratory researchers or by animal or plant specialists, unless they are also attentive observers of the natural environment.

I don't claim to have had any special interest in natural history, but as a boy I was made aware of the annual fluctuations in the number of game animals and the need to adjust the 'cull' to the size of the surplus population. I followed the family and country practice of learning to shoot with a shotgun, to stalk and shoot deer with a rifle and to fish for trout and salmon with a fly rod. Like many others before me, I came in contact with the natural world through these sports and, while learning about the conservation of game species, I began to take an interest in wild animals and their habitats.

This interest in wild animals and plants combined with

a love of countryside sports has never ceased to cause problems for those rational thinkers who convince themselves that the two characteristics are wholly incompatible. What they appear to find so difficult to comprehend is that an interest and appreciation of nature is not the same thing as an attachment to pet animals. Hunters, shooters and falconers take great care of their horses, dogs and birds, and become very attached to them, but that does not inhibit their love for country sports. It is also worth bearing in mind that it was in order to protect the game species and the forests that the hunters, shooters, fishers and foresters pressed for proper game laws, and created the protected 'chases', and the game and forest reserves and National Parks in their own countries and in their colonies. Where these do not exist, the natural environment is being rapidly eroded by so-called 'economic development' and uncontrolled exploitation.

At eighteen I went off to war with the Royal Navy for six years and then stayed on in the Navy for another six years. It was after I came ashore that I got back into country life and began to discover the fascination of being able to identify different species of birds; to know which were residents and which were migrants, and where they went during the winter or the summer. From there it is only a small step to finding out about nesting and feeding habits, about predation, and all the other influences on the breeding success of species.

It very soon became evident to me that the rules which apply to birds in a particular part of a country apply to all wild populations everywhere in the world. They all need appropriate space, sufficient food and somewhere safe to nest or breed. It also became apparent that, since migrating birds take their habitat with them, as it were, their effective conservation depends on international co-operation.

I won't go into the circumstances which led to my becoming President of the British National Appeal for the World Wildlife Fund – as it was originally called when it was founded in 1962 – a Trustee of WWF International, since renamed the World Wide Fund for Nature. It was certainly partly due to my interest in natural history, but it would be foolish to deny that a title always looks good at the head of a charity.

Whatever the reason may have been, this close association with WWF and the whole business of the conservation of nature has had a significant influence on my life and thought. It is one thing to be interested in a subject; it is quite a different matter to have to try to explain to other people that the subject is an important one and deserves to be taken seriously. I suppose I should have realised from the start that this would entail making speeches, writing articles and giving lectures and interviews on the subject of the conservation of wildlife; but I had no idea of the range of issues and thoughts that it would lead me into. Over the years a considerable mass of material has accumulated. It is this material which provides the contents of this book.

Each of the lectures and the speeches was written for a particular audience and, largely because I cannot bear to listen to myself repeating the same points over and over again, I made an effort to introduce a new argument or a new point of view as often as possible. It was the need to try to explain to others which forced me to marshal my own thoughts and to assemble a sufficient knowledge of the facts and issues. I can't say what effect my efforts have had on others, but I know that they have stretched my imagination and my own comprehension of the subject.

Some of the material has already appeared in other publications, but it was Aubrey Buxton – an old friend, a keen naturalist and among the founders of WWF – who first suggested that it might form the basis of a book on the conservation of nature. I could think of no good reason to refuse, but I did make the condition that the selection, editing and arrangement should be done by someone else. He put the idea to the Chairman of Collins, who readily agreed, and Crispin Fisher was invited to take on this task while Helen Stevenson did the difficult part of the job of putting the scheme into practice. The information contained in the boxes was compiled by Howard Loxton and Norman Tozer.

Rather than simply putting together a selection of speeches, the idea behind the editing of the material for this book was to group together excerpts relating to the same particular topic, from a number of different speeches. The general idea was to start with a selection of material analysing the human relationship with the natural world in our time. The second section then deals with some of the various ways in which the natural system is exploited for human benefit, and the factors which are causing particular difficulties for wild plant and animal life. The third section considers the influence on the natural system of the growth of the human population and the problems of managing wild animal and plant populations. The material in the fourth section looks at the decline in wild species, the reduction in wild forests and wilderness areas, and what this will mean for the human population in the future. The last section puts together some thoughts about the need for a moral and intellectual response to the crisis facing the natural environment so that the worst consequences of the human exploitation of this our only planet can be avoided, and so that future generations can be persuaded that they have a moral duty to look after what is left of the natural wonders of this world.

I

INTRODUCTION

Natural Balance
and Ecological Order

14th November 1986.
Lecture to the European Council of International Schools.
Montreux, Switzerland.

The great difficulty about 'life' is that we humans are part of it, and it is therefore almost impossible to study it objectively. It is made even more difficult by the fact that human attitudes to the living world have been largely conditioned by philosophical speculation and religious dogma developed at a time when the human population believed itself to be struggling against nature for its very survival. It therefore tends to be anthropocentric and gives scant attention to the welfare of all the other life-forms which share this planet with us.

Scientists have undoubtedly discovered a very great deal about life, but man's relationship to the natural world is not a matter of science, it is a matter of concept and conscience. The 'big bang' theory may explain to the satisfaction of physicists the origin of the universe and of our planet Earth, but it does nothing to answer such questions as What are we doing here? What is the point of existence? Is there anything beyond this life? Was the world created by a Supreme Being? Is everything that has happened since the creation part of His plan, or is it all a matter of chance? Questions which men have been asking ever since they discovered speech.

All these questions are quite reasonable. They are the product of man's ability to speak and to reason. The problem is that, as a result of man's ability to express his thoughts, there are so many conflicting answers. You can take your choice between creation and evolution; between the natural and the supernatural; between man made in the image of God and man the end of the evolutionary process; between body and brain or body and soul; between death after death or life after death or even reincarnation. You can also choose between conservation for the sake of man, or conservation for the sake of nature. Anthropocentric or altruistic?

These are philosophical choices, but it is from these choices that many others are derived. For example, when the Bible says that man shall have 'dominion' over God's creation, the choice is between understanding dominion as in 'having power over', or dominion as 'having responsibility for'.

Coming nearer to the conservation of nature, the choice is between accepting the natural system as it was created – or as it evolved – with all its perfections and imperfections, or whether we choose to believe, with Isaiah, that the natural system can be perfected. You will doubtless remember that in Chapter II he wrote:

> *Then shall the wolf live with the sheep,*
> *and the leopard lie down with the kid;*
> *the calf and the young lion shall grow up together,*
> *and their young shall lie down together.*
> *The lion shall eat straw like cattle;*
> *the infant shall play over the hole of the cobra,*
> *and the young child shall dance over the viper's nest.*
> *They shall not hurt or destroy in all my holy mountain.*

It is very attractive to believe that it is possible to do away
with all that we find unpleasant and unattractive; that pests
and diseases can be eradicated, that natural disasters,
earthquakes and storms can be prevented; that predation
can be made no longer necessary. Whatever choice you
make, the consequences are obviously very important.

For my part, reverence for nature means the reverence
for the system as it is, warts and all. If there is anything
that is to be perfected – and could be perfected – it is
human behaviour. It is perfectly possible to do without
war, without terrorism, without tyranny, without over-
population and particularly without thoughtlessly wreck-
ing the natural system by over-exploitation of what we
call natural resources. It seems quite extraordinary to me
that while we have developed such strong moral and
religious feelings about the sanctity of human life, we
seem to have failed to do anything to establish the sanctity
of the natural system on which we depend for our
existence. Whole libraries of books have been turned out
on the subject of the economics of money and the subject
is taught in every university; virtually nothing has ever
been written, or taught, about the economics of nature. I
do not accept the wholly unrealistic concept that 'being
nice to animals' is a proper substitute for an understanding
and a respect for the natural system as a whole.

Some choices depend to a large extent on self-interest.
A farmer with the exclusive use of his own land will
ensure that he keeps enough seed corn to plant for next
year's harvest. He will also keep enough cows or ewes or
sows to breed next year's crop of animals for the market.
In other words he is respecting the natural system and
practising what ecologists refer to as maintaining a sustainable yield. This is the basis of the economics of nature. It
is just as important as the economics of money, since no

human activity can be considered in isolation from the natural world which is our life support system.

In contrast to the principle of harvesting is the exploitation of what appear to be free-for-all natural resources. Apart from nations with exclusive rights to their coastal waters, most of the oceans are open to the fishing fleets from all nations which are free to exploit the natural populations of fish by whatever means are available, irrespective of the damage which the methods may have on other marine creatures and birds. Each fleet is anxious to get what it can because the fishermen know that if they don't catch whatever fish are there, the other fleets will do so. It is obviously in the common interest to limit the total catch to maintain a sustainable yield, but it is against the interests of the individual.

A more critical example is the exploitation of natural tropical forests. Governments burdened with debt see them as a source of revenue, squatters see them as covering cultivatable land and ranchers see them as potential grazing. The result is that forests are disappearing faster than they can regenerate. The choices here are between harvesting and exploitation.

The fact that some natural resources are more in demand than others also causes problems. In Scotland, for instance, deer and sheep have always been in greater demand than foxes, wolves or eagles. The latter were therefore branded as predators and every effort was made to keep their numbers to the minimum. Having removed most of the predators it then became necessary to limit the deer population to the number that could be supported on the area available. In other words, once you have interfered with the balance of nature it becomes necessary to maintain the balance by artificial means. This means that some animals have to be killed in the interest of maintaining the health and viability of the species as a whole as well as for the benefit of other more vulnerable species. Unfortunately there are many people who object to that sort of thing.

The fact is that mankind has so interfered with the balance of nature all over the world that it is now essential to take steps to maintain the balance by artificial means. Indeed, this is the basic role of the modern ecologist and all those who are concerned with the conservation of nature. It has now become impossible to attempt to maintain wildlife on earth by simple protection or non-interference.

Let me give you just one rather extreme example of one form of interference with the natural balance, as reported in the *Eastern (Airlines) Review*. The great kiskadee, a large yellow-breasted flycatcher, was introduced into Bermuda from Trinidad in 1957 to control anolis lizards. The lizards had been introduced to control Mediterranean fruit flies, but had preferred to eat beneficial ladybird beetles and parasitic wasps, the latter introduced to control oleander scale, itself an accidental introduction. Nothing now controls the kiskadees and their numbers have soared from 200 to 60,000.

The Galapagos Islands provide a different example. Visitors and settlers on the islands have introduced a number of exotic species over the years. Rats, cats, dogs, goats and donkeys have all gone feral and they have caused mayhem among the indigenous populations, particularly among the giant tortoises and ground-nesting birds. The only way to give the natural inhabitants of the islands a reasonable chance to survive is to attempt to exterminate the destructive introduced species.

Some species are obviously at greater risk of extinction than others and therefore greater efforts are made to ensure their survival, but individual species cannot be protected unless they have somewhere to exist and something to exist on. They have to have a habitat and a source of food and they have to share it with all the other species which exist in that habitat. This means that these habitats have to be protected from human encroachment and managed for the benefit of the wild inhabitants.

Ecology is not concerned with the fate of individual animals. It accepts the concept of the exploitation of surplus natural resources because that is the way the natural system works, but it must always be done on the principle of maintaining a sustainable yield.

Grazing animals depend on the renewal of the natural pastures; predators depend on a viable population of their prey. The system ordains that if populations get too big to be sustained by the resources available, sickness, starvation and death redress the balance with what we might think is cruel efficiency. The inexorable rule of nature is that if you mess up your environment you will have to pay a heavy price sooner or later.

This is a fact of the natural system that humanity has simply refused to learn – to its very great cost. Just look around the globe today and you cannot fail to notice that all the areas which at one time supported highly successful and civilized populations are either deserts or they have reverted to jungle. The reason is quite simple: they over-exploited their natural resources and they paid the price. It is naïve in the extreme to imagine that we can escape the same fate for very much longer. We are only managing to put off the evil hour by frantically digging up and using mineral resources that can never be renewed. As if that were not enough, we are polluting the atmosphere, the land and the waters with every kind of noxious substance.

The 'greenhouse effect' alone could well have devastating consequences for all life on earth.[1]

The choice in conservation is therefore between the welfare of individual animals and the maintenance of a balance which will ensure that all species of both plants and animals have a reasonable chance of survival.

Strangely enough, this duality of option is a reflection of the duality of man's brain. The left brain produces the reasonable answers after objective scientific research, while the right brain prefers the acceptable and the emotionally satisfactory answers. How often do people say 'that may be so, but I prefer to believe' or 'I like to believe . . . this, that or the other'?

This duality of brain has created great problems for modern man. When religion provided the 'satisfactory' answers to imponderable questions, and practical experience was limited to fairly simple technology, there was no great conflict between experimental fact and belief. Today the volume of scientific fact has grown to enormous proportions, and much of it is in direct conflict with traditional concepts.

This conflict produces a very difficult situation. Scientific fact is not just verifiable, it is also reproducible, which means that whole systems of engineering can be based on the certain knowledge that if the rules are followed the outcome is predictable.

It is also significant that successful engineering makes money. This is in stark contrast to the supernatural, whether it is religious or mythological. In the latter cases the truth may be equally certain, but it is not verifiable, and the outcome of following the rules is seldom predictable. It is, of course, possible to exploit magic and mythology commercially, but it could hardly be described as manufacturing industry.

While the scientist may be motivated by the desire for knowledge, the engineer is more likely to be motivated by the desire to make a living, and as the sum of the successful activities of engineers and manufacturers – within the legal and financial restraints imposed by governments – is equivalent to the national economy, there is an understandable public pressure for schools and colleges to concentrate on utilitarian subjects to the exclusion of cultural and aesthetic development. In other words, the development of the left brain is given a great deal more attention than that of the right brain.

Viewed from the practical, intellectual and reasonable aspect, this may well appear to make a lot of sense. The trouble is that neglect of the development of the right brain leaves it in a state of vacuum. The knowledge of the left brain is not balanced by the insight, judgement and understanding which the right brain should be providing.

This means that the right brain is ready to absorb the first plausible ideas that it happens to come across. The occult, obscure religious rites, parapsychology, astrology and similar attractive but irrational notions are sucked into the vacant space without any discrimination or critical faculty.

Furthermore, in the absence of an understanding of the way the natural system works, it is only to be expected that there will be an emotional reaction to the less attractive features of the system. I also suspect that the use of drugs might be seen as a substitute, or short cut, to filling the vacuum in the right brain.

You may well think that I have drifted rather a long way from my subject, but I mention all this because man's attitude to nature is partly a function of the left brain and partly a function of the right brain. It is easy enough to encourage an emotional concern for nature and the living world, it is a great deal more difficult to teach the facts of life. I know this from personal experience. I get more letters about the treatment of animals, both domestic and wild, than I do about whole species under threat of extinction.

Everyone can comprehend the idea of cruelty, very few can comprehend the extinction of a species. Everyone has views on hunting, which, if properly conducted, is a sustainable use of resources; but very few accept any personal responsibility for the pollution of the natural environment or for human encroachment and disturbance of the habitats of wild animals and plants, which causes serious and, in some cases, irreparable damage.

I am sure you are aware that for nearly 100 years there was no life at all in the lower reaches of the River Thames. I suspect there would have been an outcry if this had been due to the activities of fishermen. In fact it was due to toxic effluent from the human population and it was only cleaned up because it caused such an unpleasant smell. It took very much longer for ecologists even partially to recreate the conditions which would allow life to return to the river.

It is true that species of wild animals and plants have been becoming extinct for very many years – the dinosaurs disappeared from the earth 120 million years ago, and the reason is still not entirely understood. What modern man has failed to grasp is that the number of species under threat of extinction and the rate at which species are becoming extinct, is increasing all the time. The fate of many has already been sealed. Once the population of a species gets below a minimum viable number, or its genetic diversity is reduced below a certain level, its extinction is inevitable.

This is not happening from natural causes, but as a direct consequence of the growth of the human population and the increasingly destructive effects of the exploitation of renewable and non-renewable natural resources and of human activity in general. Typical examples of the latter are acid rain, the destruction of the ozone layer and the build-up of the CO_2 layer causing the 'greenhouse effect'.

To this you may well feel like saying 'so what?' The fact is that, in spite of all mankind's inventiveness and technological skills, it would be quite impossible for man to try to live on this planet without the life support system provided by the rest of the living world.

Many people are concerned about the risks of nuclear power stations and the disposal of nuclear waste. Even more are, quite rightly, worried that some fanatical group of politicians could start a nuclear war and create a nuclear holocaust. At the moment this is, fortunately, just a possibility. It is a risk, but it is only a potential risk. The risk to all life on earth through the irresponsible destruction of the natural world by ordinary people going about what they see as their lawful occasions, is not potential, it is actual, the damage is being done here and now, with long-term consequences just as destructive as a nuclear holocaust. Whoever said that the world would end, not with a bang but a whimper, may well have been more accurate than he expected.

The CO_2-consuming forests are being exploited faster than they can regenerate; the natural resources of the oceans are being wantonly destroyed; the waters, the land and the atmosphere are being polluted at such a rate that even the most drastic remedial measures could not be effective for very many years, and then only if the explosion of the human population could be contained within reasonable limits.

The facts are there for all to see, but they are not 'satisfactory', they are not palatable to people who have grown up in the understanding that the world was created by a benevolent merciful God specifically for their enjoyment. Therefore all must be right with this wonderful world and we are here for the sole purpose of exploiting its apparently limitless resources to make a prosperous living and then to enjoy life to the full on the proceeds.

It is difficult enough to persuade the supposedly educated populations of the developed world that this is a dangerous fallacy. How do you get the message through to communities which are living exactly the same lifestyle as their ancestors 20,000 years ago? Furthermore the job is made almost impossible by our well-meant attempts to raise the standards of living of such people. Untold economic resources have been invested in the so-called third world, particularly during the last 30 years. But what is there to show for it? There appears to be more starvation, more desertification, falling food production, deforestation, soil erosion and increasingly erratic climates. All this in addition to social unrest, terrorism and civil war brought about by ideological conflict and the pressures of rapid population increase, urbanization and industrialization. And it still goes on. Far more resources are committed to economic development than are made available for the care of the natural economy.

In one respect only can this massive investment be said to have been successful. There are now three times as many people living in this third world and the population is still rising. Such numbers could not have been sustained even 50 years ago. This is quite an achievement, but I doubt whether it was ever intended by the developers. Instead of the same number of people enjoying higher standards of living, we have achieved the situation where three times as many people are living at the same or an inferior standard to that enjoyed by their parents 50 years ago. Even to achieve this has meant a threefold increase in the demand for resources and in the populations of domestic animals, with all this means for the state of the natural vegetation.

It is perfectly possible to increase the world output of food. The 'Green Revolution' was a staggering success, but lack of food is no longer the critical factor.[2] The starvation which exists could be cured; statistically there is enough food in the world. What cannot be cured is the growing demand for resources. At its simplest, even if we could get the food to those who are starving, with what are they going to cook it? With no more natural resources than semi-arid desert, how are the products of modern technology to be afforded?

We tried much the same thing in the developed world. Our prosperity has risen dramatically since technology allowed us to abandon the agricultural way of life. But it has been achieved by creating massive urban/industrial complexes with all their problems of mass industrial employment – and unemployment – inner-city decay, social unrest, crime, drug-taking and all the rest of what we call the modern evils. Perhaps it was a fair exchange, but surely we should think twice about forcing the same sort of changes on populations which do not have the resources to maintain the standards to which we have become accustomed.

If you manage to increase the population of nomadic communities, which are dependent on grazing their flocks, there is no way you can increase the natural pastures on which these flocks can feed. Furthermore, if the human population increases, the size of the flocks is also bound to increase. The western answer is to try to settle such communities in permanent villages and to create artificial pastures. Splendid, but what about the life-style to which they have become adapted?

It seems to me that the people of this world are facing the same dilemma as the man on the desert island. He has a coconut tree, which provides him with food, but he has decided to cut it down to build a shelter. He is very comfortable in his shelter but he has just begun to notice that his store of coconuts is beginning to run out.

When we talk about economic development and the conservation of nature we have to use both our minds as well as our hearts if we are to ensure that future generations can enjoy just a fraction of the benefits of the natural world that has been left to us by previous generations. We must look at the unpalatable as well as the palatable truths. We can no longer afford to believe that learning the facts or that an emotional response are sufficient unto themselves. Knowledge and emotion have got to be coupled with insight and understanding.

The most important thing to remember is that life on earth is an integrated whole. The natural system includes the sun and the moon, the wind and the rain, the rivers and the soil, the plants and the animals, the seas and the oceans. You may be able to get away with a certain amount of tinkering, but there comes a point when one part after another breaks down and the whole system reaches the brink of collapse.

What is known as the 'catastrophe theory' suggests that everything has its final breaking point when it will suddenly, and without warning, switch from a stretched, but apparently stable situation into complete breakdown. The single purpose of the WWF, the IUCN and all the conservation organizations of the world, is to try to ensure that the natural system, that intricate web of life on this planet Earth, never reaches that point.

11th May 1982.
Speech to the Council for Environmental Conservation Conference.
London.

Conservation is a very big and complicated subject. Furthermore, the motives for conservation are primarily moral and emotional rather than strictly practical. The destruction of an historic building or the extinction of the whales, for instance, would have no practical effect whatever on all but a very few members of the world's population. There are of course certain conservation issues which also have practical significance. The effect of acid rain on inland fisheries and forestry is one example.

I think, therefore, that it is necessary to get it clear in our minds what we mean by conservation, the reasons we believe it to be important and what we should be doing about it.

In the first place, it is vital to appreciate that there are two major aspects to conservation. There is the conservation of the human environment and by that I mean all those things which have a direct influence on the daily existence of the human community. Some put a greater emphasis on one aspect than others but in general terms I would include the conservation of the best and most interesting features of the built environment, the conservation of those features of nature and the countryside that are useful and desirable for the enjoyment of people in their leisure time and the prevention of pollution to the water, the air and the land as they affect human welfare.

This is the human orientated or homo-centric view of conservation and although it might be considered rather selfish, it is certainly respectable, desirable and of course popular. Even though the primary concern is for the comfort and convenience of people, quite a large slice of the natural environment is incidentally conserved as a result of measures taken to conserve the human environment.

The other aspect of conservation is the conservation of nature and the natural environment. Whereas the human interest is obviously the motive for the conservation of the human environment, it is a bit more difficult to be precise about the motive for the conservation of nature. Take the whales. If there is no practical significance to the human population in the continued existence of the whales, why do we bother about them? It may seem a silly question to ask, but it is not all that easy to answer.

One answer might be the one given in the World Conservation Strategy, that they represent a natural resource and are, or might be, useful to mankind for some purpose or other in the future. This might be true of some, but it cannot be true of all the species of whales. But even if whales are a bit doubtful, is it really possible to include all the insects, reptiles, wild plants and deep sea organisms as potential natural resources? I rather doubt it.

The conventional theological answer might be that all plants and creatures, including man, were created or caused to be evolved, by the Almighty and therefore we have a moral obligation, as His final creation, to protect and conserve all our fellow living beings and organisms. This answer is at least comprehensive, although it leaves unanswered the problem that many species became extinct long before mankind had any significant influence on the natural world about him.

There is then what might be termed the scientific answer. This comes in two parts. First, all life forms are interesting and worth studying for the sake of acquiring knowledge; and secondly, all life forms contain genetic material which might, at some stage and under particular circumstances, come in useful. I think the answer would go on to say that as all life forms are interdependent, it is not sufficient to make a sort of catalogued collection of all existing species, because, in order for the natural world to continue its dynamic progress, the species have to exist in a natural relationship with each other.

I dare say there are other answers, or variants of the ones I mentioned; but that is the gist of the difficulty of providing a universally acceptable motive for the conservation of nature.

I think at this point I should make it clear that there is a difference between the conservation of endangered species, and animal welfare. Because the first is concerned with the survival of a viable population, whereas the latter is concerned primarily with the method of killing. As far as the whales are concerned, conservation and welfare act together, because the species are in danger. In the Canadian seal cull or in the badger situation the Welfare Lobby is concerned about the *method* used to cull the seals and to control the disease in badgers, whereas the Conservation Lobby is concerned with monitoring the numbers of seals culled and the spread of disease amongst the badger population *so the species do not become liable to extinction*. That does not mean to say that there are some people who are absolute conservationists or others who are absolute animal welfarists. They are mixed; and any discussion between the two is a discussion about issues on which some people take a stronger line on one side than the other in that particular circumstance.

Having selected a motive, the next problem is to develop some sort of reconciliation between the interests of the human and the natural environments when these conflict. The most obvious example is the human population explosion which, together with the technological explosion, is the origin of the most direct threat to the survival of much of the natural environment. Which is it to be? The unfettered right of people to have as many children as they like without any concern for the consequences? Or is it acceptable to suggest voluntary restraint for the sake of the survival of many other life forms?

Of course the alternatives are not quite as clear-cut as that, because it must be self-evident that as the human population increases so do the chances of its catastrophic collapse. Consequently, it is in the long-term interests of the survival of mankind itself to limit its total number.

7th June 1962.
Address to the World Wildlife Fund.
New York.

For conservation to be successful it is necessary to take into consideration that it is a characteristic of man that he can only be relied upon to do anything consistently which is in his own interest. He may have occasional fits of conscience and moral rectitude, but otherwise his actions are governed by self-interest. It follows then that, whatever the moral reasons for conservation, it will only be achieved by the inducement of profit or pleasure.

The moral reasons for conservation must be obvious. After all, we collect vast sums of money and go to endless trouble to preserve man-made treasures, most of which serve no practical purpose. Surely then we should also pay some attention to the living God-made treasures of this world which have a practical as well as an aesthetic value. I don't know how much Queen Victoria and Theodore Roosevelt had in common, but they were at least agreed on this point.

Queen Victoria said, 'No civilization is complete which

does not include the dumb and defenceless of God's creatures within the sphere of charity and mercy.' Theodore Roosevelt put it this way – 'The nation behaves well if it treats the natural resources as assets which it must turn over to the next generation increased and not impaired in value.'

6th November 1962.
Speech at the British National Appeal Banquet of the World Wildlife Fund.
London.

You might just as well ask why we spend so much money looking after our works of art, and our cathedrals and ancient buildings. The answer won't go into one sentence, unless you say with the mountaineer simply: 'Because they are there.' The extermination of a species of animal is like the destruction of a unique work of art. Just imagine a group of vandals going around the world every year, and solemnly taking down all the works, *all* the works, mark you, of one or two of the great masters, and carefully and deliberately destroying them.

There are many points of view about conservation, and some of them may be irreconcilable, but I still think it is worth appealing to all reasonable people to spare a thought for those animals and plants which are on the point of extinction.

Education

14th November 1986.
Lecture to the European Council of International Schools.
Montreux, Switzerland.

I am not concerned to get the conservation of nature into the school curriculum as a separate subject. What I would like to do is to convince you that all life on earth is interrelated and if any part of it is weakened or destroyed the whole system is put at risk. Therefore the conservation of nature is more than an academic subject, it is what might be described as a philosophical imperative, and, as such, it needs to permeate the whole philosophy of education both within and without the academic curriculum.

I realize that what are called the 'life sciences' cover some aspects of the subject of life on earth, but I would suggest that, like most sciences, they are 'reductionist' – the acquisition of more and more knowledge about smaller and smaller details. You cut open a frog to see what is inside and then take it to bits to see how it works. It is rather like looking inside a watch to discover the Laws of the Universe. What none of these sciences does is relate the micro-systems to the macro-systems of the natural world and universe.

24th November 1967.
Fawley Foundation Lecture.
Southampton University.

The French entomologist Fabre studied the colorado beetle with great care and discovered that for three years the larva burrows about inside an oak tree, taking in wood at one end and leaving a tunnel behind. When the time comes for the larva to pupate it makes for the bark of the tree because the beetle could not exist in the ordinary wood. The larva then proceeds to hollow out a chamber just inside the wood, but close to the bark, big enough for the beetle which does not yet exist. It covers the walls and floor of the chamber with soft wood, seals the openings and finally lies down with its head towards the exit. Were it to lie the wrong way, the beetle would not be able to turn round to get out. I suspect that it would require training up to degree standard for a larva with the mental capacity of a man to get the whole process right by deliberate effort.

However, in that part of our civilization brought about by human reasoning, virtually nothing is inherited. Children grow up physically with little difficulty, and they are capable of thought, but as far as the rational processes of the brain are concerned they begin totally ignorant. The whole basis of our existence has to be deliberately implanted: ideas and standards of behaviour, which experience and reason have found to be desirable, need to be transmitted before any new generation can play a full part in our present civilization, let alone make any significant contribution to its further progress. I sometimes feel that, like the human embryo which seems to go through all the stages of the physical evolution of the species, the human child has to go through all the stages of our behavioural evolution.

Seen in this light, I believe that there is a good case for reviewing the whole structure and content of our educational process. Not perhaps on the purely scientific or academic side, although much could be done through the use of modern techniques of communication, but on that side which is concerned with the preparation of the next generation for the conditions of our existence as we are able to understand them today. For instance, it might be found that integration into responsible adult life at an earlier stage might make things a good deal easier for those who need to undergo a long period of education and training. It would also seem particularly necessary to help students to understand and to appreciate the origin of their natural instincts and emotions, and the way they have been modified over the ages. Not so that they can be warped or destroyed but so that the best can be encouraged and those which are less suitable for our civilized existence can be kept under control.

The conflict between instinct and reason has reached a critical stage in man's affairs, largely because the explosion of facts has revealed the instincts for what they are and at the same time it has undermined traditional philosophies and ideologies. The explosion of facts has effectively altered mankind's physical and intellectual environment and when any environment changes, the process of natural selection is brutal and merciless. 'Adapt or die' is as true today as it was at the beginning.

15th March 1978.
Presidential Address to the School Natural Science Society.
London.

I am always tempted by the chance to address education-alists. I think it must be some deep-seated revenge-wish for all those years when teachers had it all their own way. I get the same sort of feeling about churchmen, but they don't seem to gather together so much, and when they do they are more cagey about exposing themselves to laymen.

I may have rubbed my hands together – metaphorically of course – at the prospect of giving this Presidential Address; but then the moment came to compose my thoughts and put them down on paper. The problem is that I have my feet in so many camps – if that is physiologically possible. To give you some idea, I did Latin and Greek at school, but I also attended schools in France and Germany and this country and consequently picked up a bit of their languages.

As I had it in mind to join the Navy, I had to take up the natural sciences which, I have to admit, neither baffled me completely nor excited me to a frenzy. Since those days I have had more personal tutorials by more distinguished scientists about more subjects in more laboratories than anyone else – at least it feels like it.

The Navy is a profession in the ordinary sense of the word, but it is a technological profession – navigation, gunnery, anti-submarine warfare and signals are all based on mathematics and physics, although when bombs are being dropped on you, or you are chasing submarines it is quite a problem to keep the emotions from interfering with the tactics and mechanics.

Then, literally out of the blue, I was invited to become President of the British Association for the Advancement of Science for its meeting in Edinburgh in 1951. There were all sorts of appropriate reasons for this, but in most respects I was hopelessly inappropriate: a 30-year-old naval officer in command of a frigate is hardly in the tradition of distinguished scientists who have held that position.

All I can say is that under the tutelage of Sir Harold Hartley the preparation of my Presidential address was the most intensive crash course in general science ever undertaken. Had the thought occurred to me that the classics and humanities were sufficient background for a well-informed and educated man in the middle of the twentieth century, the preparation of that address banished it forever. I am not suggesting that the classics and humanities are not entirely respectable and worthwhile academic subjects, they always have been and they always will be, but I am suggesting that to be without a basic understanding of the scientific method and without any appreciation of the scientific basis of modern technologies, is to be part-educated, almost intellectually crippled.

More or less specialization in scientific method and subject, or an accumulation of technical knowledge, is obviously necessary for particular professions and vocations. But to be able to take an intelligent interest in the significant events of contemporary existence in such areas for example as economics, industrial affairs and defence, a general understanding of scientific activity and the broad principles of the technologies is absolutely essential.

Perhaps I can illustrate this need in another context with a piece of personal experience. When you have heard it you may think that it has no particular relevance to the natural sciences, but the point I want to make is that unless I had had an understanding of what science and scientists were about I would neither have been able to appreciate the problems nor make even a moderately useful contribution.

I became involved in problems of the conservation of nature quite by chance. It all started when I bought a camera and a telescopic lens during a visit to Stockholm. With that camera I started taking photographs of sea birds in the South Pacific and Antarctic on my way home from Australia. This started an interest in bird-watching which in turn led to the acquaintance of other bird-watchers and naturalists.

There were several other chapters in this story until eventually an old friend of mine persuaded me to accept an invitation to become Patron of the Council for Nature; a sort of federation of Natural History societies. Not long afterwards and for totally different reasons I was invited to become President of the Zoological Society of London.

All this took place at about the time that the first agricultural chemicals were coming into widespread use and the first indications of their side-effects were becoming apparent to anyone with an interest in the countryside and wildlife. It was also about this time that a book called *Silent Spring* by the American Rachel Carson was published and the alarm bells began to ring in earnest.

Then one day the Council for Nature put on an exhibition of the work of all its members and several other interested bodies. Out of this developed the idea of a conference of all the organizations, societies and industries whose activities had some sort of impact on the countryside. The first of three conferences on 'The Countryside in 1970' took place in 1963. These in turn led to the European Conservation Year in 1970 and ultimately to the United Nations Conference on the Environment in Stockholm in 1972.

Meanwhile another old friend had persuaded me to

become involved in the project to set up the World Wildlife Fund to finance projects for the conservation of endangered species. So if I had not been conscious of the problems of nature before, those years taught me a very great deal. Apart from the actions of chemicals on food chains, the effect of pollution on life in rivers, estuaries and the sea, migration and population, I also discovered a lot about human demography, population pressures and the effects of various kinds of industrial developments on the environment. It also taught me the importance of sifting the facts from the myths and prejudices. As a matter of fact, my course of instruction was not unlike my introduction to the British Association, because it consisted in lecturing others about the threats to the countryside and the pressures on wildlife. I think most teachers would agree that you only really begin to learn a subject when you find yourself having to teach it.

It was a fascinating period as it saw the beginning of a popular concern for conservation. Up till then the interest had been concentrated in the specialist societies such as this one, each of whom pursued their activities with great knowledge and enthusiasm, but in virtual isolation from one another.

However, like all new ideas it attracted a great deal of publicity and support to begin with, only to be followed, equally inevitably, I suppose, by a sort of backlash of some quite justified criticisms as well as by those from people who professed to be bored by the whole thing. You may remember the references to European CONSERVATION Year. A rather more difficult consequence was that the very practical problem of conservation attracted a certain number of almost fanatical preservationists who tried to convert it into a sort of crusade against all kinds of imaginary enemies. Their motto seemed to be 'my mind is made up, do not confuse me with the facts'.

This was unfortunate because it so happened that the threats to the countryside and wildlife were seldom the result of intentionally malicious activities, but almost entirely due to ignorance, and you don't convert ignorance into knowledge by insult. It also created many difficulties because it is not easy to try to be objective and rational against a highly charged emotional and irrational atmosphere.

A good example of this process is the case of the Australian Conservation Foundation, of which I was President from 1971 to 1976. To begin with all went well and it attracted the support of many sensible and well-informed people across Australia. It was just beginning to make some headway in the process of educating the leading politicians and personalities in the extractive industries when what might be termed the 'extremists' staged a comprehensive coup at one of the Annual General Meetings and succeeded in taking over the whole organization.

From education they turned to confrontation and political manoeuvres which inevitably alienated the industrialists and also succeeded in putting off a good many of the Foundation's own supporters. Reason and objectivity were no longer the first considerations. As you can appreciate, I learned as much about human nature from my involvement in conservation as I did about ordinary nature.

One of the most interesting consequences of this popular enthusiasm for conservation was the way in which the word came to be interpreted. The initial object was the conservation of nature and/or the natural environment. But it seemed that this new word 'environment' was more emotionally attractive than 'nature', and it was not long before people were talking about the conservation of the environment, which very soon came to embrace everything from the view of the gas works from people's windows to the preservation of historic buildings.

Protecting wild animals from the effects of pollution and from the exploitation of their habitat inevitably has only a limited emotional appeal. The idea of protecting people against all the things of the modern world they do not like, and cuddly animals against death, not unnaturally became a great deal more popular.

Every now and then I try to point out that environment is not the key word and that the conservation of nature is by no means the same as the conservation of the human or built environment. Concern for the human environment is very important, but it is purely selfish and while I am delighted that people are beginning to realize that there is no excuse for cluttering up the landscape or the townscape with eyesores, it has precious little to do with the conservation of nature.

Perhaps the most significant aspect of this whole issue of the conservation of nature and wildlife is that it has made people take a view about something which has no direct practical effect on them personally. In that sense it is really a moral issue, and at a time when mankind seems to have become more egocentric than before, and when all discussion seems to revolve around economics and standards of human living, I do not think this is at all a bad thing. I believe that what the conservation of nature can do to make the wider public think, the natural sciences can do for children in school.

To begin with, the study of any aspect of nature is not a question of finding the right answer or a workable solution, it is a question of finding the truth. Some of the natural sciences may seem rather abstract subjects, but together they are man's own particular sciences, they hold the truth about living things and the world of nature about us.

Of course people have been trying to define truth for generations, but for scientific purposes I am not convinced that a definition of truth is all that significant. It seems to me that science is not a thing, it is a method, so that the way you search for truth is really the most important factor. If you use the scientific method you are more likely to find an aspect of real truth than if you rely on intuition or guess work or any other system.

Finding the truth is the purpose of all science and it calls for technical, personal and moral qualities. To give very simple examples: if you want to discover the truth about the structure of a fly's wing you need to know how to operate a microscope. Having got the fly under the microscope the next step is to observe, to notice significant details and to judge whether they are relevant or irrelevant. But the moral consideration is probably the most important because both technical choice and personal judgement are influenced by moral standards. Without absolute honesty and objectivity in the approach to the search for truth the results will be misleading, which is worse than not finding anything at all.

This is probably self-evident, but what may not be so obvious are the factors which tend to modify or subvert absolute honesty and objectivity in science. Perhaps the classic situation arises from an attempt to prove a strongly held theory. It is extremely difficult to set up an experiment, or to embark on a series of observations, without tending to favour the pre-supposed answer. No one can ignore a perfectly obvious and blatant failure, but it is not so easy with, let us say, marginally ambiguous results. And if the whole experiment is biased in favour of a particular solution, then ambiguous results are even more suspect.

There are also other and more subtle obstacles to finding the truth. For example, at one time religious beliefs inhibited a great deal of research. If results appeared liable to conflict with religious dogma, pressure could be applied to the research worker to drop that line and to try something else. In some cases, I can imagine that the religious convictions of the research worker himself might encourage him to accept certain evidence more readily than other, perhaps more theologically awkward, results. Teilhard de Chardin is a good example of someone who was both scientist and theologian and who spent his life trying to reconcile one with the other.

We may be inclined to believe that this whole matter was settled once and for all by the Copernicus and Darwin cases. Perhaps they succeeded in setting science free from the constraints of theological convictions, but we now have the equally damaging phenomenon of political convictions creating preconceived answers or encouraging politically acceptable solutions.

For example, fortunately for us as it turned out, Hitler would not allow nuclear research to continue because the leading research workers in that subject were Jewish. There are similar instances in Soviet Russia of which the Lysenko story is probably the best known.[3] Today we, in the so-called free world, have to face the challenge of genetic engineering and of whether to impose limits or controls on this line of research. The choice is a very difficult one as the future of all life on this planet depends upon the freedom of enquiry, yet this needs to be balanced against the moral and practical consequences of having the power to interfere with natural genetic processes and even to create quite new processes.

Preconceived attitudes are also easily acquired from other sources. Teachers, usually unwittingly but sometimes wittingly, can allow their enthusiasms to give greater or less emphasis to certain factors in their subject which can have quite important consequences. Then, as everyone knows, leaders in a subject are capable of setting fashionable theories. Elliot Smith and his theory of the diffusion of culture is an example of an eminent scientist and a strong personality who dominated the attitudes of a complete generation.[4]

It is not easy to apply rational criticism to a fashionable concept and hope to be accepted by the so-called establishment. Fortunately in science, if not in politics or economics, false conclusions never survive for very long. Even Lysenko, who had the backing of a no less powerful patron than Stalin, and consequently many supporters for his mistaken ideas, was eventually challenged and defeated.

Human nature itself also plays a part in diverting the search for truth. Scientists might not like to admit that they are liable to such emotions as vanity, jealousy, hero-worship or personal animosity, but there are too many examples of great men and great thinkers who have succumbed to these corroding influences.

I suppose the classic example was when Bishop Wilberforce challenged the conclusions Darwin had reached from his painstaking research into the evolution of species. Some of you will remember the story. During the British Association Conference in Oxford in 1860, a meeting was held to discuss the implications of Darwin's book *The Origin of Species*. During a blistering attack on the book, Bishop Wilberforce asked Huxley, who was defending Darwin, whether it was through his grandfather or his grandmother that he claimed descent from a 'venerable ape'. Huxley is reported to have replied,

> *'If I am asked whether I would choose to be descended from the poor animal of low intelligence and stooping gait, who grins and chatters as we pass, or from a man, endowed with great ability and a splendid position, who should use these gifts to discredit and crush humble seekers after truth, I hesitate what answer to make.'*

The good Bishop, whose nickname was Soapy Sam, had first allowed his preconceived ideas to cloud his judgement and, almost more reprehensible, he so far forgot his Christian principles as to try to ridicule the work of one of the most dedicated searchers for truth the world has ever known. Even if Darwin had been wrong, the Bishop had no excuse for treating him like that. The way to treat false conclusions is to prove them to be false.

The interesting point about this is that if anyone had suggested to the Bishop that he was not interested in arriving at the truth, he would have been mortally insulted.

I suggested just now that the scientific method – and life in general for that matter – requires three things: technical knowledge, personal observation and judgement, and moral standards.

I don't think there is very much anyone can do to improve powers of observation and judgement, except perhaps with practice and by emphasizing how important they are. They require a certain talent which is given to some and not to others. Technical knowledge, on the other hand, can be acquired up to quite extraordinarily high standards. This is one of the principal responsibilities of schools, colleges, universities and a mass of other organizations. The argument is not about the possibility of imparting technical knowledge, the argument is simply about what technical knowledge is necessary for anyone hoping to earn a living, or simply to exist and appreciate life in a modern, technically advanced community.

The problem of moral standards is a great deal more difficult and their importance within the education process is frequently overlooked. Yet the experience of every civilization has been that the general standards of honesty, integrity, compassion, manners and personal behaviour, which are acquired during the education process, are far more significant than the standards of academic achievement. A society of brilliant barbarians would soon end in chaos in any society. Even the less brilliant can all become clean, honest and well-mannered and that would be a big step towards a more civilized society.

It's easy enough to recognize the need for absolute honesty and integrity in relation to science, but I don't believe that you can switch moral standards on and off at will. I don't believe that it is possible for someone to justify lying in one context and not think of bending the truth in another. There cannot be any such thing as a separation within the individual between public and private morality. People try of course, but it is liable to create intolerable tensions and they usually get found out in the end anyway.

In the same way there cannot be any separation between religious truth and scientific truth. They may well be dealing with different aspects of the subject, but it is not possible for something to be true in a scientific sense and not true in a religious sense. Equally, theology cannot claim something as true which can be disproved by scientific methods. That is not to say that theology is prevented from claiming that it can provide a theory to explain things for which science can provide no explanation.

Indeed I would suggest that theologians and scientists are each aiming at the same goal, although taking different routes, and they need to recognize this if we are ever to restore a unity of outlook on all moral problems. If there is to be any separation between theology and science, then let it be decided by function and not by forcing people to choose between conflicting demands. Absolute standards of honesty are required by science, but there are many other moral issues in human life which are the proper concern of theology.

The relevance of all this to the study of the natural sciences is that I believe they form an essential link between pure science and the human experience. They are subjects of interest in themselves but they are also the foundation for understanding man's place in the universe. It seems that we have become so dazzled by what we take to be our own creative genius that we have neglected, or forgotten, or ignored the infinitely complicated web of nature which sustains our very existence.

This suggests to me that of all the subjects taught in school, the natural sciences, and natural history in particular, are the ones to which all children should be exposed. After all, humanity is a part of what de Chardin called the biosphere – in other words the living world and its environment – so there really is a good case for giving natural science the same level of importance as literacy and numeracy. If you come to think of it, a lot of people survive without being able to read or write or do arithmetic, but no one has thought of a way of living without a body. It is rather a sad commentary on our contemporary priorities that of all the functions of our bodies, the only one that schools feel it worth bothering about is the reproductive system.

A background of knowledge of the natural sciences is essential for all technologies and most vocations and professions. However, I believe that the case for natural history, and particularly biology, as a core subject can be justified from a number of points of view. Each of us is a component part of living nature anyway, and furthermore, unless we can learn to understand living organisms we are very unlikely to be able to understand ourselves or anything of man's situation. It can be justified from the scientific point of view because natural history teaches the basis of the scientific approach to all subjects and also because it emphasizes the decisive value of observation and judgement.

I think it can also be justified from the moral point of view because in contrast to mathematics, for instance, which depends on accuracy and only admits right and wrong answers, the right answers in natural history, namely the truth, can only be found by the deliberate choice of rigorous honesty and objectivity. Furthermore, it provides an introduction to the origins of instincts and behaviour and to the challenging moral complexities of the conservation of nature, the use of animals in scientific research and biological engineering itself.

I believe there is yet another justification which might be described as the intellectual point of view. I think it could be argued that the creative arts belong to the world of the imagination but the imagination cannot spring into instant being; there has to be some input before it can begin to function. Many children have a latent talent for music or painting, for instance, but for this talent to become creative it needs the resources of the imagination and the stimulus of inspiration. And not only for creation.

Imagination also plays a big part in the appreciation of works of art.

However I am not suggesting that the study of natural history in itself can provide either the input for the imagination or the direct inspiration to create, but I am suggesting that in the process of studying natural history in the laboratories and particularly in field studies and expeditions, the imagination is exposed to natural beauty which has been the source of inspiration for generations of creative artists. In this age when such a large proportion of the population lives in an urban, industrial environment the need to expose the imagination to the wonders of the natural world is, I believe, greater than ever.

So in thanking the Society for inviting me to be its President in its 75th year and giving me this splendid opportunity to work off my revenge wish, all I want to do is to encourage the Society to develop the techniques of teaching natural science and to take full advantage of the great debate on the content of education to press the claims of natural history in particular as one of the core subjects of any future system.

The Role of the World Wildlife Fund and the International Union for Conservation of Nature and Natural Resources

27th May 1981.
Presidential Speech to the 20th Anniversary Reception of the World
Wildlife Fund.
Wembley.

To be President of WWF International is a daunting and challenging prospect and I only accepted the invitation because I have witnessed the interest in conservation and the enthusiasm of so many people for the work being done by WWF and IUCN.[5] There are one million regular donors to WWF all over the world.

WWF has been going for twenty years; for the first fifteen years under the distinguished and energetic Presidency of my senior colleague Prince Bernhard of the Netherlands, and then since 1977 under Mr John Loudon's considerable managerial talents, and I would like to pay a very warm tribute to his leadership and dedication to the WWF. I have no illusions about how difficult it is going to be to follow them as President. They have been, and I hope to be, assisted by a number of eminent and influential people from many countries who give up a great deal of time as members of the Board of International Trustees. The Headquarters staff, first under Dr Fritz Vollmar and then under Mr Charles de Haes, have given dedicated and loyal service in the day-to-day management of the Fund's affairs. There are in addition 26 National Organizations which have raised the funds and been responsible for a number of important projects within their own countries while also making vital joint contributions to projects in countries which cannot call on sufficient resources to meet all their own needs. The conservation of nature knows no national boundaries, it is equally important to all people whatever their race, their colour, their religion, their culture or their wealth.

Before this great idea was launched 20 years ago, there was no central funding organization for the conservation of wildlife. Today, 20 years, $55 million and 2,800 projects later, WWF can look back on its achievements with considerable satisfaction. But that feeling of satisfaction does not mean we can sit here in the belief that everything is all right. $55 million in voluntary subscriptions is quite impressive, but when you consider that it is roughly equivalent to the sum spent on advertising in the national newspapers in Britain in 1980 alone it doesn't really amount to very much. The wonder is that this sum has enabled us to achieve so much. If anything, the threats to wildlife and to the whole natural world are even more serious and even more dangerous today than they were 20 years ago. Therefore we cannot possibly afford to relax our efforts.

We start the next 20 years with a sound organizational infrastructure. The partnership and joint headquarters with the IUCN, with its 480 members, is well established, flourishing and effective. The WWF Headquarters administration is funded by earned income and by the support of the 1001 Group, initiated by Prince Bernhard, and therefore no money sent to International Headquarters for conservation projects has to be used for administration. There are not many major charities that can make such a claim and I think we should acknowledge this vital contribution by the members of the 1001.

The Conservation Monitoring Centre is established at Cambridge next to the offices of the International Council for Bird Preservation. I was able to visit both offices quite recently and I can report that work on the Red Data Books on Endangered Species, which provide the essential information for many conservation projects, is progressing satisfactorily. The fact that these offices are next to each other makes the work of both of them that much more effective.

Crucial to the whole campaign for the conservation of endangered species is the establishment of four global conventions for which WWF and the IUCN can claim much of the responsibility. They cover Trade in Endangered Species, Wetlands, Migratory Species and the World's Cultural and Natural Heritage.

Many governments have already decided to adopt these conventions, but they need to be signed by many more. Even more important is that ministers and civil servants have got to believe in them and ensure that they are implemented. We must not let governments believe that they can simply sign on the dotted line and then quickly forget to do anything about it. I am sorry to have to say that there is mounting evidence that several governments of wealthier countries, in spite of a lot of talk and promises, have done little in practice to control the extremely damaging trade in endangered species. As long as markets exist in the affluent countries there will always be people prepared to do anything to satisfy the demand.

I have great hopes that the 'TRAFFIC' organizations set up to monitor international trade in wild animals and their products, will begin to make a significant impression before long. I am sure that it will be one of the most effective means of bringing pressure to bear on those governments which, so far at least, have not fulfilled their obligations.

We must never lose sight of the fact that our prime purpose is the conservation of endangered species and the protection of their habitats. This is for one very good reason – no other organization is doing this work and, though the control of trade may seem rather unexciting, if it is vigorously implemented it could well be an extremely valuable contribution to conservation worldwide. Successful conservation depends on realistic and effective programmes and not on dashing off after fashionable and emotive causes which are so often totally irrelevant to the conservation of wildlife.

A most important development has been the collaboration between WWF, the IUCN and the United Nations Environment Programme, with help from the Food and Agriculture Organization and UNESCO, in the production of the World Conservation Strategy. This document sets out clearly and unequivocally the purpose of conservation and traces practical guidelines for the benefit of all international agencies, national governments and voluntary organizations committed to the conservation of nature. WWF International and National Organizations must never relax their pressure on governments, and other conservation bodies, to work out and to put into action specific strategies for their own particular situations. The headquarters staff of WWF and the IUCN at Gland are only too ready to offer help and advice.

Even so the most difficult aspect of conservation still remains to be tackled. The information about what needs to be done is available in the Red Books, the strategy for how it should be done has been worked out in the World Conservation Strategy and some of the means by which it can be done, such as the international conventions, are at hand; it now remains to convince people in positions of responsibility and authority to find the money and to take the necessary action; in fact to get on and do it.

The question which we in WWF have to settle is how we are best going to help to achieve the objectives of the Strategy.

In the first place I believe we must recognize that there are three separate and distinct aspects of conservation. There is the technical and scientific side, which embraces the assessment of risks and dangers and all decisions about the measures needed to ensure the survival of threatened and endangered species and their habitats, and the conservation of nature as a whole. This aspect is highly specialized and I believe that in all such matters WWF should rely on the expert advice of our partners, the IUCN. This leaves WWF with the responsibility for considering the financial, practical, social, political and administrative aspects of conservation projects and for establishing priorities within the limits of our resources.

Secondly, all conservation projects and public relations programmes need to be paid for. It is therefore the primary function of WWF to raise the money for the projects proposed by the IUCN, as well as for its own public relations programmes and for the services it must provide for National Organizations.

The methods adopted to bring conservation to the attention of the public and to raise funds are twofold. There are special international appeals launched by WWF International for specific purposes. These have included 'Operation Tiger', 'Save the Rhino', 'The Seas Must Live' and probably most important of all the 'Tropical Rain Forest Campaign' to begin next year.

At the same time the National Organizations run their own appropriate campaigns and raise funds for their own conservation projects, but they are also expected to make a contribution, through WWF International, to IUCN sponsored projects in other parts of the world.

Thirdly, there is the public relations or propaganda side. This is to do with getting the conservation message across and creating new attitudes among the public in general and, in particular, among opinion makers, politicians, public administrators, managers, professional people and the media. Unless these people come to realize that the conservation of nature requires practical programmes and effective measures we will never make much progress. Appeals to their emotions are not enough. They must be made to see that the conservation of nature is as vital to the health and well being of future generations as proper sewage disposal or the supply of clean water.

Needless to say, our most important propaganda task is to get the message across to the younger generation, and we must use all possible means including teachers in schools and colleges, youth organizations, volunteer lecturers, television programmes, the specialized media and of course the national conservation bodies themselves.

It so happens that philanthropists have been concerned with education for very much longer than they have worried about conservation. Consequently there are a number of major charities and foundations which cannot support conservation projects as such, but which might well be persuaded to support education in conservation. In fact WWF-UK has already started a special Educational Trust Fund in order to attract donations from such organizations and so far it has raised £250,000 for educational projects.

Getting the conservation message across by all these means might be described as a political activity, but only in the sense that conservation is a subject of public interest. It is definitely not political in the party or ideological sense. Indeed the conservation of nature is probably one of the very few causes which finds support among all sections of the community of all shades of political philosophy in all parts of the world. In fact I suspect that it is a cause about which even the churches can agree.

Propaganda for conservation is therefore a proper and extremely important function of WWF. It is for this reason, in addition to raising money, that we need to encourage the formation of National Organizations and to provide them with all the help, information, advice and support that we can give them. They are in the front line of the conservation propaganda battle and we must see to it that they never lack for ammunition. National Organizations for their part must be seen to be active promoters of the cause of conservation in their countries and that in turn will help them to become even more effective fund raisers for international projects.

There is therefore a very great need for the closest possible co-operation and integration between the IUCN, WWF International and the National Organizations. This has become progressively more important as the conservation movement has developed in range and scope. I propose to make this integration my first priority. We will not be able to achieve our objectives until WWF is so organized that we can make the best possible use of all the talent and goodwill which is at our disposal in so many parts of the world, and of the technical information provided by IUCN and its members.

There is one other matter which we need to take into consideration. WWF is committed to the conservation of nature through measures which allow both animal and plant species to survive as viable populations. However there are also a number of very closely related, and publicly very important subjects, such things as animal welfare, population control, pollution of the human urban environment, the human enjoyment of nature and other particular environmental issues. In my opinion there are many excellent national and international animal welfare organizations and specialized pressure groups and I think it is best for all concerned if we recognize a division of responsibilities. I hope we will keep in the closest contact with these organizations so that we can co-operate whenever the need arises and always show each other mutual respect and understanding. But I believe that WWF must get on with its work as we understand it, just as animal welfare groups should get on with theirs. No organization can be all things to all people. The task for which WWF was established is quite challenging enough without going off to tilt at every windmill that appears on the horizon – and in any case the resources are not available.

I have not spoken about the general need for the conservation of the world's natural environment or about the problems and difficulties which face WWF and IUCN in attempting to meet this need. But I do just want to say this: we are facing an extremely dangerous situation, the natural environment is being assaulted as never before and the survival of whole ecosystems and their flora and fauna is seriously threatened. The human population continues to explode and its sheer size demands more development, more space and more exploitation of the resources of nature. If it continues to increase for much longer the natural world will be destroyed and the collapse of the human world will inevitably follow.

The idea that humanity is struggling to survive against

the forces of nature is ridiculous. There are occasionally some very unpleasant natural disasters but in spite of them the vast and growing human population together with its technical progress has given mankind a dominant influence on all life on earth. Sooner or later anyone committed to the conservation of nature is bound to be asked that simplistic question, whether it is right to worry about plants and animals when so many people are starving. It is not a choice between man or nature, it is a question of man and nature, for if we fail to look after the natural world mankind is unlikely to survive either. As if the human population explosion, poaching, agricultural encroachment, exploitation of forests, erosion and disturbance due to public access and commercial exploitation of wild resources were not enough, we have to sit watching impotently as human violence, wars and revolutions cause untold damage to wildlife. People worry about the effect of pollution, but just think of the man-made ecological disasters in such places as Uganda, Afghanistan and South East Asia.

In the face of the rising human flood and the violent and irrational behaviour of so many of its members, the resources available to WWF are pitifully small. They are certainly better than nothing, but if we are to do more than just put a finger into the hole in the dyke we must set about raising funds with redoubled vigour and purpose. In the end it is not how much ink is spilt, or how many miles of film are used or how many hours of talk or the number of receptions that counts. The only criterion that matters is the figures in the WWF accounts. There it is that you will find the evidence to indicate the commitment of nations to conservation.

II

EXPLOITATION OF THE NATURAL SYSTEM

It took about three and a half billion years for life on earth to reach the state of complexity and diversity that our ancestors knew as recently as two hundred years ago. It has only taken industrial and scientific man those two hundred years to put at risk the whole of the world's natural system. It has been estimated that by the year 2000, some 300,000 species of plants and animals will have become extinct, and that the natural economy, upon which all life depends, will have been seriously disrupted.

The paradox is that this will have been achieved with the best possible intentions. The human population must be properly fed, human life must be preserved and human existence must be made safer and more comfortable. All these things are obviously highly desirable, but if their achievement means putting the survival of future generations at risk, then surely there is a pressing obligation on present generations to apply some measure of self-restraint.

In this Chapter on 'The Exploitation of the Natural System' there are grouped together comments on the consequences of the unrestricted pursuit of certain human activities. Some of the consequences, such as pollution by human and industrial effluents, are obvious enough. Others, such as the provision of water supplies for human consumption, are so desirable in themselves that it is difficult to accept that they might have any undesirable impact on the natural system.

Forestry activities might have been included in this chapter, but, apart from certain particular practices such as extensive clear felling or the monoculture of exotic species, most forests are allowed to re-generate or are re-planted. The issue of the exploitation of the world's remaining natural forests is dealt with under 'Victims of the Unnatural System'.

Intensive Farming

1st October 1980.
The Fairfield Osborne Lecture.
New York.

Paradoxically it has been the success of the medical and agricultural sciences which has made the human population explosion possible. It is one of the laws of nature that any population will increase to consume the food and the space available unless checked by disease or famine. The conflict arises because while everyone with the slightest spark of humanity clamours for more food to feed the growing number of under-nourished people, conservationists are loud in their protest about modern farming methods, and the reclamation of wilderness areas for agriculture. But attacking agriculture is rather like blaming 'man'. Who identifies with agriculture? It is an abstract concept, useful maybe for economists and for the civil servants and scientists who work in government departments of agriculture, but I doubt whether farmers and landowners feel that it applies to them personally, and I am quite certain that the very large number of peasant and subsistence farmers in the third world are completely unaware of the argument anyway. In any case farmers have their own conflict of interest to resolve. They have to farm for profit, or to put it the other way, they obviously cannot afford to farm at a loss. Therefore they are unlikely to be sympathetic to any form of wildlife which in fact, or in their belief, is likely to reduce their yields.

It is not that farmers do not understand the principle of conservation. After all they practise it all the time. They have to keep back seed and breeding stock for next year's production; they have to provide a habitat for their stock, and they have to feed it. In fact many of them take a lot of trouble to make life possible for a large number of wild creatures without great cost to themselves; and at the same time they make their farms that much more interesting and satisfactory places to live on. There are any number of examples in many parts of the world of farmers who do just that and still manage to thrive economically.

But the conflict of interest becomes much more intense in the so-called developing countries. To the eyes of conservationists the great natural rain forests are objects of beauty and delight and the habitat of a vast range of plant and animal life. They are also vital components of the world's climatic conditions and the carbon-dioxide/oxygen cycle. But to the governments of these countries, struggling with internal hunger, poverty and unemployment, with external debt and with a plethora of well-meaning advisers and foreign aid programmes, the forests represent wealth in a fairly easily convertible form. Anyone who feels like persuading them otherwise needs to proceed with caution and much tact.

3rd February 1986.
Address to the European Management Forum Foundation Symposium.
Davos.

We have been hearing a great deal about poverty and the shortage of food in certain parts of the world. It is usually assumed that this is due to insufficient wealth and insufficient food. It would be equally true to say that no system can support a population bigger than a certain size; anything greater means that the share of the available wealth and food becomes smaller for everyone.

To give you an example. In March last year I visited several countries in the Sahel region of West Africa. This area has suffered from outright drought or below average rainfall for the last fifteen years. Yet during that period both the human population, as well as the population of domestic animals, increased by a third. As a result the natural pasture has been seriously degraded and the tree cover severely reduced by the increased demand for fuel.

What little economic development has taken place has been quite inadequate to compensate for the population growth and the destruction of the meagre natural resources.

Natural resources are of two kinds. Renewable (they can be regrown), and non-renewable (only extracted once).

Apart from recycling, there is not much we can do about conservation of the non-renewable resources. The earth only has a finite supply of conveniently available mineral resources and it is just a matter of time before they become exhausted. Needless to say, the bigger the world's human population, the sooner these resources will have been used up.

Renewable natural resources are a different matter. Provided we manage them properly, and we succeed in achieving a reasonable limit to the human population, we could go on exploiting them indefinitely. The trouble is that all the evidence suggests that we are consuming next year's seed corn. It is estimated that India has lost half of its forests in the last forty years. It is said that Madagascar has lost half its tree cover in the last ten years. To replant on such a scale is unimaginable.

It is true that agriculture is doing very well in some parts of the world, but there is a limit to its productivity, and every new acre brought into cultivation means another acre denied to wild species.

It is a misconception to believe that the world's human population would be able to exist indefinitely on domesticated species of plants and animals. The genetic variation would become too limited to be able to provide insurance against the risks of disease and genetic uncertainties.

Human survival depends on the conservation of the genetic diversity of the wild species of plants and animals.

4th June 1982.
The Chancellor's Lecture, Salford University.

In the second World Conservation Lecture at the Royal Institution in March this year, Mr Emil Salim, the Minister of State for Development, Indonesia, made these comments.

1. *'Rapid population growth will increase the pressure to produce more food. This requires more agricultural investment in land resources which gives rise to a situation where cultivatable land is rapidly running out and whatever land is now under cultivation is approaching the limits of its carrying capacity. Agriculture will therefore tend to become more dependent on capital inputs such as fertilizers, insecticides and mechanization with all the environmental and social problems that these imply. Moreover the need for more capital inputs into agriculture might put the cost of food beyond the reach of the poor.*

2. We must therefore continue with both development processes and conservation efforts simultaneously, and these are indeed the twin objectives of our national efforts for two basic reasons. First, that a sustainable environment will in turn sustain our development process, sustain the society in which our children and their children will live, and secondly, that man's dignity and the quality of his life also depend on the environment in which he lives.'

13th April 1961.
Seventh Graham Clark Lecture to the Institutions of Civil, Mechanical and Electrical Engineers.
London.

Luckily in supplying humanity's basic need of adequate food the resources are not only renewable but the area which can grow them, as well as the quantity from a given area, can be substantially increased by modern engineering and scientific methods. This is particularly fortunate because no country can hope to reap the benefits of industrialization without a sufficient and cheap supply of food for both the rural and urban population. Secondly if the world's food resources had a known limit at this time the tremendous increase in the population of the world would pose an insoluble problem. As it is things are difficult enough. Dr Norman Wright of the FAO has estimated that the world population will have grown from 3,000 million in 1961 to 4,000 million in 1980 and 6,000 million in 2000. On the basis of bringing the average world diet to a reasonable level by 1980 he has suggested that we must increase the world's cereal production by 33 per cent and the world's production of milk, meat, eggs and fish by not less than 100 per cent. By the year 2000, the figures are a 100 per cent increase for cereals and 200 per cent for animal products.

I want to introduce a few more revealing statistics. The Commonwealth fraction of the world land is 23 per cent and its fraction of the world population is 24 per cent. Even though Britain has the highest population density, 68 per cent of the Commonwealth population is in India and Pakistan. Out of a total Commonwealth population of 682 million no less than 56 per cent are employed in agriculture – 5 per cent of Britain's, 12 per cent of Australia's and 71 per cent of India's. The really interesting part of that comparison is that agriculture, forestry and fishing employ 5 per cent and are worth 4 per cent of the gross domestic product in Britain. Australia employs 12 per cent which produces 17 per cent, whereas in India 71 per cent of the population only produce 47 per cent of the gross domestic product. This shows very clearly that great strides are possible in agricultural productivity.

As I have said, for the time being we are also fortunate that the land area for agriculture can be increased. In fact 44 per cent of the Commonwealth land area is either unused, built-on or wasteland. This figure needs to be qualified, however, because one fifth of the undeveloped land surface is too cold, one fifth too arid, one fifth is mountainous and one tenth has no soil. This leaves about 30 per cent as potentially cultivatable and gives some idea of the scope for bringing deserts, equatorial forest and tropical grasslands into production, and the tremendous contribution which engineering can make to agriculture.

Four things are needed to stimulate and increase agricultural productivity:

1. Extend the area under cultivation which generally means the provision of water in dry areas, the removal of

water in swampy areas, and the control of pests, diseases and weeds.

2. Increase the productivity of the soil by applying more nutrients. This is the first impact of industry proper upon agriculture because plants need fixed nitrogen, phosphorus and potassium, which have to go through some sort of industrial process before they are usable.

3. Better equipment for use on the land so that together with the increased use of fertilizers the output per acre can be substantially improved. In the industrially developed countries very sophisticated machinery is needed to increase the output per man. In the less developed countries the emphasis should be on improved design of simple instruments. Remember the groundnut scheme which prompted the remark 'Give us the job and we will finish the tools.'¹

4. A system of agricultural organization which will make it worthwhile for the rural population to grow food for sale. This includes the organization of land tenure, proper transport and marketing facilities and a comprehensive advisory service.

It is no use attempting any or all of these things without taking human nature into account. These points may be self-evident to an outsider but you cannot, without much suffering, force human nature to accept a complete change – even for the better – of the basis of its existence overnight. The art in this case is to reconcile the interests of the individual with the interests of the state.

Much progress has already been made and if we learn from the successes even more rapid progress is possible in the future.

It is only necessary to look at the tremendously high agricultural productivity of New Zealand to realize what can be done under very favourable conditions. The Gezira cotton scheme in the Sudan is an excellent example of all the points I mentioned,[2] while the huge irrigation schemes in India and Pakistan are both an encouragement and a warning. Warning because the early schemes have given rise to water-logging and salinity which are taking as many acres out of production as new schemes are bringing in. New methods of irrigation, drainage and tube wells are now beginning to overcome these problems. I visited the Land Reclamation Laboratories in Lahore and gained some idea of the complexity and magnitude of their task. In addition to recovery of previously productive land there are plans to bring a further nine and a half million acres in Pakistan into production by irrigation. Even so the race between the growth of population and the provision of additional resources is desperately close.

Even without mechanization or increasing the area under cultivation productivity can be very greatly improved by the application of fertilizer and trace elements where necessary. This operation, however, depends upon the cheap and therefore industrial production of fertilizer which in turn depends upon cheap power. For this purpose the natural gas fields of Pakistan are most convenient as they supply both the power and the raw material for fertilizer production.

Taking all this into account it is rather sobering to find that the Commonwealth share of the world's food production is not very impressive. Of the basic foods only rice, 24 per cent, barley, 20 per cent, and mutton, 23 per cent, are in proportion to our population. All the others are way below 20 per cent of the world's output. Coarse grains are only 9 per cent, pigmeat is 5 per cent and wheat 14 per cent. This is in spite of the fact that many areas in Commonwealth countries regularly produce two and sometimes three crops per year already.

From what I have said I need hardly emphasize what is expected of engineers for agriculture especially in the less developed countries.

The next stage after food production is food preservation. There are one or two old-established methods of preserving food but generally speaking the whole technique of food preservation is due to modern engineering methods. It has even gained the title of food technology and not even the homely and old-fashioned smoking and curing methods have managed to escape the food engineers.

Food technology is already most important in keeping out undesirable organisms. It is going to become even more important in tropical countries which are rapidly developing huge concentrations of population. This whole field of the preservation and distribution of food is wide open to the engineer. Freezing, canning, curing, spray and freeze drying, ionizing radiation and every kind of processing are all engineering problems.

Lastly, I think it is generally recognized that our harvest of food from the sea is still very under-developed. Both the methods of extraction and control could be considerably improved by modern equipment and scientific study.

The point seems to be that it should not be necessary to disrupt what has proved to be a reasonably satisfactory human structure merely so as to take advantage of modern technology. The important aim is to raise standards of living and to release the poor from a subsistence farming level of existence.

The vexed question in this theory is that big farms, properly managed, are inevitably more efficient than smallholdings, yet the antipathy to large properties remains just as strong. The fact is that in the industrialized countries farming has become an industry with the land as its workshop. In this connection the reforms which have been carried through in parts of the Near East within the last few years are extremely interesting. Existing cultivated land has been redistributed and the owners of uncultivated land have been given inducements to bring large new areas into cultivation. This means that the area is going to need the most sophisticated agricultural machinery and techniques in order to bring these large areas into production. In addition it will need suitable machinery for the smaller farmers so that they can continue as independent producers at a reasonable level of efficiency.

We are only slowly beginning to recognize that the development of farming machinery of all kinds, based on an independent source of power in the form of the internal combustion engine, has completely changed the pattern of country life. We have allowed technology to make it increasingly difficult for the relatively small owner-occupier farmer to make ends meet. Yet many laws of inheritance and taxation tend to keep properties small. We have transformed farming into an industrial operation where size and turnover alone make it possible to invest in the expensive overheads and capital equipment.

This may be the right way to do it from the point of view of efficient production, but to force this pattern on the closely settled agricultural communities of the Eastern world would mean a most tremendous upheaval in their way of life and an almost insuperable problem in sorting out ancient systems of land-holding and inheritance. I suppose this could be done by forcing collective farming techniques on these people, but I think a more humane solution is to adapt our technology to their needs and to their environment. This would mean the development of small, cheap machines for individual farmers and deliberately designed equipment for produce collection, processing and marketing.

Some changes in the traditional marketing system are inevitable but this is probably best done through a much wider development of farmers' co-operatives, both for purchasing supplies of such things as seeds and fertilizers and for marketing the produce. Where these co-operatives exist, such as in India or in the Gezira cotton schemes in the Sudan, they have been conspicuously successful.

On the subject of bringing new areas into agricultural production, it is true that modern machinery has made it possible to displace the jungle and drain swamps, but these are the last remaining areas which can sustain wildlife in any quantity. They may be the easiest and most obvious areas to bring into production but it can only be done at the cost of destroying creatures who have had every right to share this planet with us for a long time and should continue to do so. The areas we should be looking at are the deserts, both natural and man-made. The challenge to technology may be greater but in the long run their reclamation will do less harm to our general environment, and more good to our general existence.

8th November 1967.
Speech at the Conference of the Royal Agricultural Society of the
Commonwealth.
Toronto.

Mechanization enters into every operation to do with the use of land for agriculture. Land reclamation, irrigation, drainage, cultivation, cropping, handling, storage and finally transport are all dependent upon engineering and mechanical equipment. In fact, apart from pesticides and fertilizers, the one single factor which has been responsible for increased agricultural productivity is mechanization.

In those countries where mechanization has been introduced, about 4 per cent of the population is capable of producing from 60 to more than 100 per cent of the national food requirements. In many other countries 70 per cent of the population engaged in cultivation cannot do as well. What would happen in India, for example, if the cultivators dropped to 4 per cent hardly bears thinking about, but that only means that mechanization must be introduced in a way most suitable to Indian conditions.

In the case of India and other areas with similar problems, irrigation and drainage can bring more land into cultivation and the mechanization of handling, storage and transport can make an important contribution. Only the mechanization of cultivation and cropping would have to be tailored to the needs of small farmers. This is as much a social, economic problem as the simple mechanization of agriculture.

The very powers of engineering cause their own problems. For instance, land reclamation is eroding the wild areas of the world which are the last refuges of our fellow creatures. We can well ask whether it is in man's long-term interest to wipe out the remaining wildlife. One can also well ask whether it is in man's long-term interest to go on increasing the world population.

There are two sides to the solution of the problem of malnutrition, more food or a stabilized population.

Then the very intensity of cultivation which mechanical devices make possible raises the problem of maintaining the soil fertility.

Water is another problem. Human civilization is demanding more and more fresh water and agriculture has one of the most urgent claims on the available supplies. Draining swamps, diverting rivers, creating reservoirs and all the other things which engineers do with water, are changing our whole environment.

There are really two sides to engineering as it affects agriculture. There are first those structures, techniques and machines which are directly used by producers. By that I mean the machinery and installations which individual farmers acquire and control themselves. This in itself is a rapidly expanding area. If combine harvesters immediately spring to mind, they are only the thin end of the wedge. Virtually every type of soil has its specialized cultivators, virtually every crop has its specialized harvester; every process for the application of fertilizers, weed and pest controls have their own machines from aircraft to knapsack tanks. Milking arrangements, the preparation and distribution of fodder and the collection of manure are all in the process of mechanization, if not automation.

The other side is perhaps even more important. It might be called the infrastructure of agriculture. This includes everything from a regional reclamation and irrigation system, to the equipment and installations required to collect, process and store agricultural produce. Not least important is the transport network and specialized transport equipment which alone can decide whether remote areas can become profitable producers.

Another important part of this infrastructure is the invention and development of new machines and installations. Much of this is done by the manufacturers but there is also a need for research establishments to look even further ahead. Needless to say nothing can happen without a strong corps of suitably trained technologists and technicians, conversant with the farmers' practical problems and requirements.

We all know only too well that city people have always maintained a rather patronizing air of superiority over the bumbling and old-fashioned farmer. I am not going to suggest that city people are totally lacking in intelligence so I can only assume that this superiority is due to simple ignorance. The fact of the matter is that farmers in the technologically advanced countries have progressed just as fast as any other industry. In fact, any comparison in the increase of their productivity with other industries shows that they have done far better than average. Indeed, in some cases productivity has grown faster than the city gentlemen planned for, with the anomalous result that in some areas there is too much food in a world suffering from a chronic shortage.

All this has come about as a result of active co-operation and understanding between farmers, scientists and engineers. Between them they have shown that they can transform agriculture and it is quite apparent that the possibilities for the future are even greater. I believe it is only by attempting to become aware of these possibilities that we can ensure that the changes which engineering is bringing about are not only profitable, but, as far as we can tell, are in the long-term interests of mankind.

18th February 1981.
Address to the All-Party Conservation Committee.
London.

Less than fifty years ago the weight of any piece of machinery that could be used on the land was limited by the strength and the speed of the horses required to move it. Diggers, bulldozers, drain-laying and earth-moving machinery of any kind were virtually non-existent. Today large tractors can pull eight furrow ploughs in almost any conditions. Combine harvesters can cover 3–4 acres in one hour, and every kind of fertilizer, herbicide, fungicide and pesticide can be sprayed on the land or the crops at almost any time of the year from the ground or from the air.

15th November 1983.
Address to the Bangladesh Federation of Chambers of Commerce and Industry.
Dhaka.

The fact is that virtually every commercial and industrial activity makes some sort of impact on the natural environment. It may be through the economic exploitation of wild populations, such as fishing or extracting natural forests. It may be through the production of raw materials from the land, usually known as agriculture. It may be through the extraction of minerals and the effect which that has on the natural countryside. At the other end of the process, it may be through the pollution of the air or the land or water as a result of the discharge of effluent and waste.

It may be that no single one of these activities in isolation has a dramatic impact. But taking them together, compounded by the effects of growing human populations, expanding cities, more transport facilities and greater demand for food and water, we should not be surprised that the rate of erosion of the limited areas still left to wild populations of plants and animals is rapidly reaching disastrous proportions.

As a result arable cultivation is more clinical, the individual fields are bigger, and all the rough corners and patches on the farm have been brought into cultivation.

The latest idea is to try to make use of otherwise useless vegetation such as bracken, or harvest heather instead of burning it, to convert it to usable energy. Both the harvesting and the conversion are only becoming possible as a result of technological progress.

The invention of barbed wire made stock-proof hedging unnecessary, and the machinery exists which can grub up redundant hedges, and with them much valuable habitat, without difficulty. But even if the old hedges are left, they have a limited life, and many of them are reaching an age when they are beginning to die off. Unless there is a need for shelter or some form of windbreak, there is no economic justification for the expense of replanting. Hedgerow trees, which are such a feature of our country-side, are gradually disappearing as they die of old age. Young self-sown trees are not given a chance to grow because it is not easy for a man driving a mechanical hedge-cutter to avoid them. We are now trying out a system of attaching labels to the young trees to help the drivers.

Diggers and drain-layers have made it possible to drain marshes and wetlands and to control river banks. Sea walls can be constructed and salt-marshes brought into cultivation.

The final question comes in two parts: are we making any real headway? And what are the long-term prospects?

It was to emphasize this aspect that WWF and IUCN set up the Development for Conservation Center in Washington. Its purpose is to monitor development projects as they work their way through the major aid organizations to ensure that their potential impact on the natural environment is appreciated and taken into consideration before, rather than after, the plans are approved. I am glad to say that the World Bank among others is willingly co-operating in this process. This is applying on an international scale the principle already adopted in many countries of assessing the environmental impact of projects. A good example is in Ceylon, now Sri Lanka, where there is a major irrigation scheme development, because thanks to the eradication of malaria about 30 years ago the population of Sri Lanka has trebled. And the result is they have got an enormous extra number of mouths to feed and people to employ.

30th April 1986.
Lecture to the Royal Society of Arts.
London.

It is very easy for chemicals and effluent to get into the food and water systems and this can have quite unpleasant consequences for all consumers whether human or wild. I remember years ago when the arsenic-based chemicals were being used in agriculture, and it was quite evident that they were extremely poisonous, people complained that they were harming the birds and the animals. The reply was, 'Oh well, as long as you use the right equipment and you follow the instructions on the packet you will be all right.' However, when you read the instructions on the packet, it turned out that the chap applying it had to be dressed up as if he were entering a chemical warfare zone, and you were also told that the field had to be kept clear of any livestock for the next 48 hours – not always practical.

Certain products used in agriculture, such as pesticides, herbicides and fungicides, can create havoc by interrupting food chains and by causing physiological changes in species which, among other things, can affect their capacity to breed. There is now evidence that the run-off of agricultural nitrogen is beginning to affect human health. There is also growing evidence that oxides of nitrogen and sulphur released into the atmosphere from the combustion of fuels are the cause of acid rain which affects both trees and water courses.[3]

The consequences for wildlife of all this progress can easily be imagined. Nesting sites have gone, sources of food have been destroyed, habitats transformed and disturbed. While it is undoubtedly possible for these consequences to be mitigated, indeed many farmers and land owners make great efforts and spend a lot of money in trying to compensate for them, the economics of agriculture are such that yields, output, productivity and margins, in spite of grants and subsidies, are all-important for the economic survival of most farmers. There are those who claim that farm improvements should be more closely controlled by legislation. The irony is that many of the offending improvements are actually financed by government grants. The pressure to produce as much as possible – and this includes bringing as much land into cultivation as possible – has been a matter of government policy for decades, and oddly enough it is achieved more by high rates of taxation than by high rates of subsidy.

Extract from 'Men, Machines and Sacred Cows', published in 1984 by Hamish Hamilton, London.

In one case an irrigation programme was designed to try to produce more agricultural land. The project was engineered straight off the drawing board; then all the conservation consequences became apparent, so there had to be a very major re-think. And as you can imagine a lot of pride was hurt, and a lot of people said, 'You can't do this; it's too late; it's going to spoil the scheme.' If that project had gone through the process of environmental impact assessment, the scheme would still have gone through, but the damage that it was liable to inflict – and which it is hoped will now be avoided – would have been worked out before it had got off the ground.

The apparently obvious solution to a problem is seldom, if ever, the right solution. One very good reason for this is that problems are never as straightforward as they appear to be at first sight. Furthermore, in the real world, neither the problems nor their solutions bear any obvious relationship to what the theorists and ideologists believe them to be. This may well be due to the fact that ideologies create problems where none exist, and that theoretical solutions are largely based on good intentions. Unfortunately experience shows that good intentions are not the same thing as good solutions. For instance, the obvious solution to the problem of cracking a nut may be to hit it with a sledgehammer. The intention is undoubtedly good, but the solution is demonstrably bad.

Water Resources

1st October 1980.
The Fairfield Osborne Lecture.
New York.

Water seems to have the most extraordinary effect on engineers. They either want to keep it in dams and reservoirs, or they want to drain it away to the sea as quickly as possible. The single-mindedness with which hydro-electric engineers, municipal water supply engineers, irrigation and drainage engineers go about their business is most impressive, and I am quite sure that they do not set about their work with the sole intention of destroying the natural environment and removing the habitat of wild species. It is not that they do not care, it is simply that many of them just do not know, and a little politely offered information is more likely to have an effect than a military confrontation. After all, they are just as capable of understanding the value of conservation as any of us present here today – and as far as I know there may well be some enlightened water-engineers in this audience.

Ten years ago the River Thames in London was virtually lifeless. Today it is once again being used by migratory fish and much other wildlife. This rehabilitation of a severely polluted waterway is a good example of what can be achieved, at quite a modest cost, by understanding and co-operation between conservationists and various specialist engineers.

The difficulty is that engineers have to reconcile the

demands of their communities with the needs of nature, and that is not at all easy when angry rate and tax payers are demanding service for their money. As a matter of fact I would not be at all surprised if the same people who complained about inadequate water supplies and sewage services were also devoted conservationists giving both time and money to persuading 'man', or perhaps 'agriculture', to mend their ways.

In these days of threatened energy shortages it is tempting to suggest that more power should be produced from sources of ambient energy, such as windmills, solar collectors and further hydro-electric developments. Some of the schemes might be quite harmless and some even beneficial to the natural environment, but others could be extremely damaging. It is impossible to generalize and in the end the decisions will depend on the good sense and judgement of the individual engineers and administrators responsible for the generation of energy. Both their good sense and their judgement would naturally be vastly improved if they had a greater understanding of, and sympathy for, the problems of nature.

It follows from this that at some stage during the formation of those engineers who are going to specialize in the branches of engineering which are liable to have an impact on the natural environment, they need to be made aware of the damage their developments are capable of inflicting on eco-systems and habitats.

4th June 1982.
The Chancellor's Lecture, Salford University.

Water is probably the most important element in conservation. It gives life to all plants and creatures, but once polluted it carries all sorts of effluents great distances; it dissolves chemicals, and it deposits noxious materials in marshes and estuaries where they stay and remain as a poison. It can be dammed by hydro-electric works, pumped up from aquifers and moved about for irrigation. As a result water tables can be lowered or raised. Irrigation without drainage can raise the water tables so much that, first, salts crystallize on the surface, and later the land becomes waterlogged. An example of the consequences of changing water systems is the Nile after the construction of the latest high Aswan dam, the Nasser dam. Every year the low-lying lands beside the Nile used to be flooded and fertilized by a new layer of silt deposited during the floods; the river then dropped and drained the land. The dam has provided massive quantities of water for irrigation, and hence increased production. But it has also regulated the river so that it remains at about the same level all the year round, and this has raised the water table so that large parts of Cairo are threatened with rising damp; and I am told that the feet of the Sphinx are suffering from efflorescence.

A further consequence has been the raising of the level of the salinity of Lake Qarun, south-west of Cairo. But perhaps the most worrying consequence is that the constant deposit of silt, which formed the Nile delta, is no longer being brought down by the river, whereas the erosive action of the Mediterranean waves continues, so that the coast is being eaten away and the extensive coastal marshlands are now threatened with inundation from the sea. From all this you will appreciate that conservation is involved with an endlessly interlocking system of causes and effects, far too complicated for the enthusiastic amateur.

11th March 1987.
Address to the Joint Meeting of the All-Party Group on Population and Development and the All-Party Conservation Committee.
London.

There is a rather naïve faith abroad that all can be made well by bringing more land under cultivation, planting trees, digging wells and making dams. It is very difficult to make trees grow where there is little or no top soil. Wells naturally attract stock and farmers from all around so that the well soon becomes the centre of a circle of desert.

Dams inevitably flood the bottom of valleys where the best agricultural land and the highest concentrations of people are usually found. Unless the water running into the dams is reasonably clean, they tend to silt-up at an alarming rate and strange things happen downstream.

Irrigation sounds attractive, but it does not always work quite as well as the theorists expect. In any case the social problems of converting people who have grazed stock for thousands of years into agricultural labourers on collective farms are not easily overcome.

It is claimed that dams can be used both for irrigation and for generating electricity. This is usually a fallacy, since you need a full dam to make electricity and the only time there is a surplus of water is during the wet season when the farmers have the water anyway. Let me quote from a recent issue of *New Scientist*:

'In the process of "developing" the State of Sarawak, the
Malaysian government plans to undo in the rainforest what
nature has taken centuries to achieve – by building a dam.
As the Bakun hydro-electric project gets under way, and
the massive dam fills up, 4000 million cubic metres of water
will submerge the settlement of Long Bulan and its farms,
together with farms belonging to fourteen other settlements.
Shifting cultivation, an ancient and integral part of the
indigenous people's way of life, will vanish from the area.
Hundreds of square kilometres of virgin tropical rainforest,
with its wealth of flora and fauna, will also go under.'

The claimed benefits are power and irrigation. Power for
industry and irrigation for agriculture. I somehow rather
doubt whether the people of Sarawak will greatly appreciate these supposed economic benefits.

Evidence from the Hoover Dam in the United States,
the Aswan Dam in Egypt, the Volta Dam in Ghana and
dams in Thailand suggests that, for all their vaunted
economic benefits, they have caused even greater problems for the local populations and the environment. The
trouble is that the disadvantages only become apparent
years after the dams have been built. This emphasizes that
environmental impact assessments of such projects are
vitally important and need to be taken very seriously
indeed.

The assessment of the economic advantage alone is
patently not sufficient. If human and ecological disasters
are to be avoided, I believe it is even more important to
assess the social and the ecological impact of such projects.

Exploitation of the Natural System

23rd November 1973.
The 4th Jane Hodge Memorial Lecture, The Institute of Science and
Technology.
Cardiff.

Perhaps the most famous and intractable example is the case of Lake Pedder in south-west Tasmania.

The lake lies in an area which until recently was almost impenetrable and which had been declared a reserve. The gist of the problem is that the Hydro-Electric Commission designed a very ambitious scheme which involved building a dam and creating a vast storage reservoir. Unfortunately Lake Pedder was included in the reservoir area which meant that the original lake was to be flooded under an extra thirty feet of water. Biologists pointed out that certain insects and plants were unique to the peculiar beach structure of the original lake and were liable to be exterminated, but it is much more difficult to stir up emotion about an insect than some appealing furry animal or spectacular bird. The main objection therefore is that the development has seriously modified an area of untouched natural beauty.

Fundamentally, this is a clash between the human desire to preserve a certain area in an undisturbed form on the one hand, and the determination to harness natural resources to human needs on the other.

19th May 1985.
Address to the Council Meeting of the World Wildlife Fund.
Divonne, France.

I think there can be little doubt that WWF enjoyed its widest public exposure during the past year at the time of the Hainburg dam issue. In 1985 it had been the intention of the Austrian Government to construct a dam and hydro-electric installation on the Danube some 50 kilometres east of Vienna. The effect of the dam would have been to prevent the flooding of an area of primeval woodland swamp known as the Auen, into which the Danube floods when the mountain snows melt. The Auen are among the last remaining flood swamps of this nature in Europe and they contain very rich populations of a wide variety of increasingly rare plant and animal species.

It was a very sad dispute, because warnings had been sounded on every side about the popular opposition to the scheme, on practical as well as on environmental and conservation grounds. I think that the most interesting feature of the dispute was that it was eventually resolved in the peaceful atmosphere of a court of law. WWF-Austria took out an injunction against the Austrian government and to everyone's relief it was granted.

I do not think there is any desire to celebrate the outcome as some sort of victory. In any case it would be premature. It is much more important that it should have the effect of persuading others in positions of authority that conservation issues need to be taken seriously. As the natural environment gets progressively eroded, so these issues will become more urgent.

Property Development and Transport

Extract from an Article in 'The Observer', London, 1984.

At the root of the problems of the countryside is a conflict of interests. To the farmer and forester it is a source of income; to newspapers, it is the place that provides the raw material for their newsprint; to the extractor of minerals, it is a part of an industrial process; to builders and manufacturers, it is a place for houses and factories; to the transport industries, it is a place to build roads, canals, railways, airports and harbours; to the energy industries, it is a place for power stations, dams and refineries; to the leisure industry, it is a place for sport and recreation; to the casual visitor, it is all too often a place to drop rubbish before going home; to wild animals and plants, it is home.

To reconcile all these vested interests is not going to be an easy task, but it would be a step in the right direction if these conflicts of interest were at least to be more widely recognized.

Down to Earth

28th October 1970.
Address to the 'Countryside in 1970' Conference.
London.

The whole problem revolves around the use we make of our environment, and particularly of our land surface. We must find places to live, places to cultivate, places to work, places for transport and places for recreation.

Somehow or other, we have got to so manage and allocate these places that there is also room for the wild plants and animals who share this planet with us. Furthermore, we have got to manage our day-to-day existence so that we do not damage the land with litter, or by pollution, over-use or exploitation. I believe that we have made quite an impressive start in the counteraction against thoughtless and ignorant exploitation.

It is just as well to recognize that land is wanted in the social interest for housing and recreation, in the economic interest for national or individual prosperity and in the interest of nature for the populations of wild plants and animals. In some cases – but not all that many – certain places may be used for more than one purpose.

Some people are concerned with planning, others with land use for parks and reserves, with recreation or the reclamation of derelict land, with refuse disposal, pollution control, management of water resources or with nature conservation and preservation. There is also the promise of greater government involvement and responsibility through the new Department for the Environment.

This is all very encouraging, but it is just as well to recognize the fact that we are not all interested in the countryside for the same reason. In every case, except for the conservation of nature, we are prompted by self-interest, either for profit or for pleasure. There is no point in deluding ourselves about this. Indeed, I doubt whether we shall ever be able to take any effective measures in the fair allocation of the different sorts of places we all want unless we have a clear idea exactly why they are wanted.

We have got to get used to the idea that each group is going to approach the subject from the point of view of self-interest, although individuals may find themselves supporting different interests at different times. Even naturalists drive cars. Having accepted that, we must go a step further and recognize that compromises have to be reached. Disagreement is inevitable, but the groups must go on meeting because we have simply got to hammer out answers to problems which are going to affect all life in these islands for generations to come. No matter how awkward the choices, we have to see they are made and made with intelligence.

4th June 1982.
The Chancellor's Lecture, Salford University.

To many people there is an apparent clash between conservation and development. Of course it is not really a clash at all, because the consequences of development without any thought of conservation are self-evident and equally conservation without development is really unthinkable; therefore the two have to go together and in order to inject more awareness of conservation problems among developers, IUCN has established a conservation development centre at its headquarters in Switzerland, and the World Bank has made it clear that in future it needs to be satisfied that the environmental impact of development projects must be assessed before, rather than after, the project has started.

Down to Earth

2nd March 1978.
Opening of the Annual Conference of the Tree Council.
London.

Everybody wants motorways, but no one wants them anywhere near where they live. And the same, strangely enough, is true of the countryside. We want a new social structure but we also want to keep the countryside created by the old structure. Landscape, after all, reflects a certain way of life and through the ages the landscape has changed with the changing social and economic conditions.

10th March 1977.
Conference of the Capital Cities Lords Mayor.
Brisbane.

What makes it all so perverse is that no sooner have people rushed in to enjoy the glamour of a city and made a success, than they promptly rush out again to settle in the suburbs, where they long for the peaceful and uncomplicated life of the country. This suggests that in order to get the best of both worlds, more medium-sized cities would be preferable to just a few vast and slowly strangling conurbations.

No sooner had the migration of workers and administrators swollen the cities to an intolerable extent, than the road system was struck by a transport explosion brought on principally by the personal motor car. To be more exact it is an explosion every evening and an implosion every morning as the suburban dwellers commute to and from their homes and places of work.

Exploitation of the Natural System

4th June 1982.
The Chancellor's Lecture, Salford University.

Conservation is for nature and wildlife and for that part of our environment which we admire, but there is no way of protecting a living landscape from change. A new landscape is inevitable and in my opinion we should be concentrating on those parts over which we have practical control; such things as public land, Forestry Commission forest, parks, open spaces, motorways and railways, inner cities, rivers, rubbish tips, recreation areas, power lines, coastline and above all the urban-rural interface.

After all, more people are exposed more frequently to these neglected areas than have ever seen the beauty spots. There is so much we can do, and the resources are so limited, that it seems to me to make better sense to attack the black spots and the eyesores and to leave the people who live by the land to exercise their own taste and judgement. They are, after all, no less responsible or intelligent than urban members of committees and commissions, although of course they are much more sensitive to economic pressures. Let the foresters and the farmers get on with their jobs and they will do their best for the landscapes they know and live with and love. They have looked after it for a thousand years and I can see no reason why they should not be trusted to go on doing so within the contemporary social and economic constraints.

18th February 1981.
Address to the All-Party Conservation Committee.
London.

More damaging than industry is the vast transport network of roads and railways. Apart from preventing the movement of animals across country, the people who use them must account for the death of vast numbers of such animals as hares, rabbits, deer, badgers, hedgehogs and young birds every year.

On top of that, it has been shown that there is a significant deposition of lead from engine exhausts on roadside plants and even some way into adjoining fields. As with the accumulation of the persistent agricultural chemicals, so the lead works its way up the food chain until it is sufficiently concentrated to cause illness and death.

In recent years public recreation has seen significant developments. Long abandoned inland waterways are being used by pleasure craft of all kinds and, unless they are specially equipped, there is inevitably an effluent problem. In addition, the disturbance and the mincing action of propellers and the effect of their wash on the banks virtually prohibits the survival of any form of wildlife on whole stretches of water.

On land the constant tramp of feet in what would otherwise be a wilderness or quiet area causes erosion problems, although the disturbance to local wildlife is probably more important. I see that the Royal Society for the Protection of Birds has issued a Bird Watchers' Code of Conduct with exactly this problem in mind.

27th May 1982.
Reply to the President of the British Property Federation.
London.

It is suggested that property owners, landlords and developers are endangered species and in much the same situation as the Asian Elephant. It should be borne in mind, however, that the elephant is in danger because its environment is being destroyed or, to put it the other way round, the jungle where it lives is being taken for human use.

It is suggested that there is a clash between development and conservation. I think it is important to get the definitions right. There are two areas where development can take place – urban areas and green field areas. Equally there are two aspects of conservation – concern for the built environment, by which I mean historic buildings and other man-made structures; and the natural environment, which is that part of the countryside that is either more or less wild or where man manipulates natural processes through agriculture for his own benefit.

The causes of the conflict between development and conservation should be fairly obvious. First, and most important, is the human population explosion. The more people there are, the more resources they require and consequently the more development is needed. Second, is the technological explosion which has massively increased the technical infrastructure per head of the population. For example, water, sewage, electricity, transport, communications and leisure opportunities all have an impact on this natural environment.

As a developer the first thing to do is to establish whether the development is likely to affect the built or natural environment, bearing in mind that any effects on the natural environment are usually indirect. The next move is to commission someone to prepare an appropriate environmental impact assessment before, rather than after, the final plans are made. The same object will be achieved, but with less fuss.

In my experience of the conservation movement, most of the damage is done by ignorance rather than by malice or greed and by lack of foresight rather than by any technical incompetence.

Anyone with a reasonable understanding of modern life appreciates that the development and redevelopment of property is an absolutely essential service, and I can only hope that the British Property Federation will succeed in its efforts to improve the environment in which development takes place, to make its performance more efficient and to foresee the consequences of its activities.

25th November 1970.
Address to the Annual General Meeting of the National Council of Social Service.
London.

We have come to think that everything is solvable in economic and material ways, and suddenly we are pitchforked into this very unpleasant situation of having to make a moral judgement. We have got to decide from a purely moral or religious point of view what we are going to do about this situation, our situation, the human situation, in this country and in the world as a whole. From a practical and economic point of view we can say, 'Well, let's do away with all the wild animals, let's get rid of all the pests, let's cut down all the forests, let's develop every acre of land, let's occupy it for our benefit.' This is the material and economic answer. The problem that we are facing now is something rather more difficult. It is a moral and religious problem as to how we see our situation on this earth. We are now up against it, we have got to make a very important decision.

Changes may be better for some – and for many they are, of course, better, don't let's delude ourselves. I think the technological advances have generally been reflected in a much better standard of living for a very large number of people. Don't let's mistake that for one moment, but don't let us forget that all changes also cause casualties. So that instead of screaming abuse at each other, let's at least recognize that we are all confused and that we are all looking for ways to come to terms with this new situation. It's not only the young who see anomalies and injustices in human nature and in the structure of human society. I think a lot of people see these difficulties and these contradictions. They are new problems or perhaps just old problems in a new form, and as a result the old solutions are no longer effective.

Some may feel that we are living through the disappearance of what many held very dear, but you've got to look on the other side of it; there is also an opportunity to build for the future, just as so many of our most satisfactory towns and cities have developed over the ages, not by being destroyed, but by the contribution which each generation has made to their life and to their structure. I am sure that we can capitalize on the best of the existing features and build new structures which will be better adapted to the present and future situation.

Pollution

24th November 1969.
Address to the Edinburgh University Union.

Pollution is a direct outcome of man's ruthless exploitation of the earth's resources. Experience shows that the growth of successful organic populations is eventually balanced by the destruction of its own habitat. The vast man-made deserts show that the human population started this process long ago. There are two important differences today. In the first place, the process has gone from a walking pace to a breakneck gallop. Secondly, we know enough to appreciate what is happening and the need to take care.

There have been isolated areas of pollution ever since the first coal mines washed coal dust into the rivers and the first metal smelting works gushed every kind of toxic waste into the air and into the water. You have only to look at the derelict land in the South Wales valleys to see the destruction caused by those operations. These were prophetic demonstrations of the danger of pollution, but they were local and they were accepted in the interests of progress and employment. No one recognized them as awful warnings of what was to follow. Today pollution has reached a level of intensity which very few even dreamed about as little as twenty years ago.

Let me briefly outline the main causes. First, industrial pollution. This can take the form of atmospheric effluents which damage or destroy living organisms, reduce visibility and solar radiation or, through the interaction of rain, pour down various toxic or destructive chemicals on land and sea. Manufacturing industries are also enormous consumers of fresh water and in many cases the water-borne effluents can be extremely destructive. Even when the water is treated and returned as clean it certainly does not have the same characteristics as the raw water had before it was used.

Then there are various forms of pollution caused by the production of energy from both thermal and nuclear power stations, motor vehicles, trains, aircraft, ships and the rest. Nuclear waste products are a problem in themselves but all these sources are responsible for growing atmospheric pollution. On top of that the power stations are immense consumers of cooling water and the effect of this is to raise the temperature of the water of the rivers, estuaries and coastal sea water to an extent which sharply affects the whole biological structure in the area.

Probably the most dangerous kind of pollution is caused by pumping raw untreated sewage straight into rivers or into the sea. From time immemorial man has dumped all his waste products into the nearest river. With today's immense urban populations this has resulted in every major river in the world becoming nothing better than a convenient open sewer with all the consequent hazards to health and to all the other living creatures who also inhabit this earth.

There is pollution by industrial products. This can vary from virtually indestructible plastics, whether sheets or containers, to all the derelict and no longer usable things such as old motor cars and bedsteads, in fact the whole vast and growing problem of domestic waste disposal.

Pollution is no longer a matter of local incidents; today it has the whole biosphere in its grip. The processes which devastated the Welsh valleys a hundred years ago are now at work, over, on and under the earth and the oceans. Even if we bury all this waste underground, there still remains the risk that toxic materials from chemical reactions will be washed out and into underground water courses. If ever there was an area of research closely related to human welfare it is the problem of the safe disposal of waste and effluents.

The fact is that we have got to make a choice between human prosperity on the one hand and the total well-being of the planet Earth on the other. Even then it is hardly a choice, because if we only look for human prosperity we shall certainly destroy by pollution the earth and the human population which has existed on it for millions of years. We talk about over- or under-developed countries; I think a more exact division might be between the under-developed and over-populated. The more people there are, the more industry and the more waste and the more sewage there is, and therefore the more pollution.

At the moment it seems as if pollution is too remote for most people. Indeed, judging by the amount of rubbish of all kinds which the average citizen chucks out of his car or dumps on every available parking, camping or picnic site, he is unlikely to feel any concern for pollution on a grander scale. Every year, on the public roads in certain parts of the country the situation gets worse. Every parking place becomes a stinking dump of rotting rubbish. I see this myself every season and I can only assume that the same applies all over the country. What astonishes me is that so many people continue to ignore the possibility that anyone else might like to use the same site after them. This is not special pleading, because I have no wish and no need to use these sites myself; but I do know that there are any number who will be using them. It is this general lack of concern for the future which worries me, particularly as precisely this situation exists on a global scale.

If the world pollution situation is not critical at the moment, it is as certain as anything can be that the situation will become increasingly intolerable within a very short time. The situation can be controlled, and even reversed; but it demands co-operation on a scale and intensity beyond anything achieved so far.

I realize that there are any number of vital causes to be fought for, and I sympathize with people who work up a passionate concern about the all too many examples of inhumanity, injustice, and unfairness; but behind all this hangs a really deadly cloud. Still largely unnoticed and unrecognized, the process of destroying our natural environment is gathering speed and momentum. If we fail to cope with this challenge, all the other problems will pale into insignificance.

1st October 1980.
The Fairfield Osborne Lecture.
New York.

The waste and sewage disposal authorities have to resolve a particularly awkward conflict of interests. Their problem is that treatment costs money; and no elected body ever wants to ask for more money than the community believes to be absolutely necessary. If the community is unaware of the dangers of discharging untreated sewage into rivers or estuaries, it is unlikely to press local governments to spend money on treatment works. The inhabitants of the smaller and more rural communities live rather more closely to these mundane affairs, and are consequently more likely to appreciate the problems than the people living in the great metropolitan conurbations, most of whom are blissfully unaware of the damage caused by the disposal of their wastes and sewage. Furthermore, pollution control is a relatively recent idea. Consequently it is not easily accepted by organizations which have been able to do as they pleased for a great many years.

This also applies to many industries, but here again not all industrial processes produce pollution, and even different companies performing the same processes do not all produce the same amount of pollution. In some situations the effluents can be discharged without damage, while in other cases companies, of their own volition, take appropriate measures to prevent their effluent doing any harm. The difficulty today is to identify the particular company which is causing damage and then to discover which individuals in that company have the necessary authority to take steps to prevent it. Then again, in some cases these individuals will accept the conservation argument and do something about it; in other cases they may not be so co-operative. It is therefore important to devise a system which penalizes those responsible for the damage and so provides an incentive to control pollution.

All industrial companies have to live with the market system so there is no reason why the price mechanism should not work in such cases, provided of course that a cost can be put on the damage done to wildlife and the natural environment.

Even more intractable is the international pollution conflict. The River Rhine is an international waterway flowing through many different countries, each of which applies its own, and in some cases that means no, pollution control. The power stations on the east coast of Britain have high stacks to carry the effluent clear of the population. However, the prevailing wind in from the south-west and much of the sulphur dioxide comes down and affects the forests of Sweden.

Then again, something like 70 per cent of all the pollution of the sea is by oil caused not by accidental spillages, grounding or collisions, but by the deliberate cleaning of ships' tanks. The damage this does to sand beaches, sea birds and marine mammals, and to the spawning and hatching areas of fish and shellfish must be very considerable and obviously calls for severe penalties.

4th June 1982.
The Chancellor's Lecture, Salford University.

One hotly debated issue directly attributable to the development of industry is the question of the build-up of carbon dioxide in the atmosphere, due partly to the increased output of the gas from the urban industrial complexes and the reduction of the forest areas capable of converting it into oxygen. The consequences could be what has been described as a greenhouse effect. This could result in raising the average temperature and melting the ice-caps, which would affect some 6 per cent of the population – that's 11 million people of the United States alone. (Greenhouse effect – see also p.289.)

Industrial development involves virtually every profession. In agriculture, for instance, it was soon discovered that persistent pesticides were creating havoc among wild species. Chemists went back to the drawing board, or wherever chemists go, and a new generation of selective and degradable pesticides and herbicides was developed. This represents an important improvement. But the problem of the run-off of agricultural chemicals, including fertilizers, into waterways is still very serious. Even the new chemicals themselves are causing problems, because they have the effect of taking out important links in the food chains of wild populations.

Dams, hydro-electric works and irrigation schemes can be constructed in such a way that the natural water courses and the wild animals and plants that are dependent on them are not totally deprived of water or habitat. Many industrial processes, particularly mining operations, produce toxic wastes of various kinds. Given the will or the legislation these can be controlled. Indeed in many cases the control of such wastes can make the whole process more efficient.

One of the most worrying consequences of the large-scale burning of sulphur-rich oil fuels in factories and power stations has been the phenomenon of so-called acid rain. Lakes, rivers and forests in Scandinavia and Canada have been badly affected, and the latest casualty is the Black Forest in Germany where trees in the worst affected areas are dying at an alarming rate.

It might be argued that all this is due to greed for profit and the insatiable appetite of consumers, but this is not the whole story. Central and local governments bear a large share of responsibility. Lack of understanding of the consequences of their actions, ineffective or inconsiderate legislation, the inability to enforce legislation, political prejudice, civil unrest and terrorism, all have a dramatic impact on the natural world. Not to mention the laudable social ambition for economic development.

The fact is that virtually every commercial and industrial activity makes some sort of impact on the natural environment. It may be the economic exploitation of wild populations, such as fishing or extracting timber from natural forests. It may be through the production of raw materials from the land, usually known as agriculture. It may be through the extraction of minerals and the effect which that has on the natural countryside. At the other end of the process, it may be through the discharge of effluent and waste. It may be that no single one of these activities in isolation has a dramatic impact; but taken together and added to the effects of growing human populations, expanding cities, more transport facilities and greater demand for food and water, it is not surprising that the rate of erosion of the limited areas still left to wild populations of plants and animals rapidly reaches disastrous proportions.

I mention this because I cannot believe that any individual businessman would like to feel personally responsible for the extinction of any species of wildlife. But he may well be so without knowing it. I also happen to believe that it is not only possible but vitally necessary for the long-term welfare of future generations of the human species, that economic development takes place without causing irreparable and irreversible ecological damage. I hardly need to remind you that a great number of people depend, to a very large extent, on the healthy productivity of natural forests and wild-life. Development is obviously essential but considerate development can only be achieved if the captains of industry – the decision-makers in business – comprehend the consequences of their decisions and make conscious and deliberate efforts not to cause any permanent or irreversible damage to the natural resources which are so essential to future generations.

3rd February 1986.
Address to the European Management Forum Foundation Symposium.
Davos.

My impression is that a growing number of complete industries have begun to realize that they can make a significant contribution to the conservation of nature by self-regulation. A few years ago the Greek ship-owners got together with the WWF and the IUCN to develop a code of practice to prevent their ships causing oil and waste pollution at sea and in harbour. This has been a great success and we hope that it will be taken up by other fleets.

In the United States a new private non-profit organization has been set up under the name of 'Clean Sites, Inc.' It is a union of major chemical interests such as Dupont, Monsanto, Exon and the Chemical Manufacturers Association together with conservation groups including WWF-US and the Conservation Foundation. Its purpose is to monitor and arrange the cleaning up of sites of toxic waste.

There is a rather unusual case here in Switzerland. It seems that 50 per cent of all the coffins used to be made of obeche wood from West Africa. This point was made in a television broadcast, launching the WWF/IUCN Tropical Rain Forest Campaign in 1982. As a result the largest Swiss coffin-maker, Rudolf Egli AG of Beromunster, announced that it would switch to local poplar and the Swiss Timber Association has offered to support WWF in its campaign to discourage the use of endangered tropical hardwoods.

There are signs that the fur trade is also beginning to realize that it is in its interests to support national government legislation designed to conserve the wild species on which their trade depends. I very much hope that other trades and industries which make use of such natural raw materials will soon come to the same conclusions. Without such involvement the poachers and the illegal traders will most certainly destroy their trade in the very near future.

And lastly, I am very glad to say that more and more companies are making direct contributions to WWF for conservation projects, either by donations or through joint promotions. I say companies but companies can do nothing unless their managers so decide. It is very evident to us that many more managers appreciate what conservation is all about and are prepared to commit their companies in its support.

A good example is the joint promotion with the FIAT company. Five European WWF offices are engaged in joint promotions with FIAT to raise funds for the conservation of nature. Last year a special project to mark the production of the millionth FIAT Uno looks like raising thousands of lira for conservation in Madagascar.

And that is not all. I cannot give you the exact figures, but it would be true to say that the great majority of the board members of WWF International and its 24 National Organizations are active businessmen who give us the benefit of their advice and expertise and, in many cases, donate large sums of their own money as well.

Recent years have seen a remarkable development in the partnership between business and the conservation organizations to achieve more effective protection of the natural environment. I hope very much that this partnership can be further strengthened and extended in the future.

The fact is that there is no inherent conflict between industry and conservation. It all depends on the comprehension and understanding of individual managers. Companies are entitled to do what they can to maximize profits for the sake of their shareholders and workers, but this cannot be done regardless of any other factors. Responsibility for limiting the damaging effects of any aspect of company operations on the natural environment, is just another factor to be taken into account in the same way as such things as the health and safety of the employees or the quality of the products or the truthfulness of advertisements.

It is no more likely that every company will have a sensible conservation policy than that every company will be managed with honesty and integrity. What should be possible is that every honest and responsible manager should have a sufficient understanding of the facts of the natural environment to enable him to manage his company with a proper regard for the long-term well-being of the whole living world.

30th April 1986.
Lecture to the Royal Society of Arts.
London.

Industry Year was launched in this room just about three months ago and it was an initiative taken by the Royal Society of Arts. The purpose of the campaign, of course, is to create a new and a more sympathetic attitude towards industrial companies and activities in this country. The idea is to persuade people that employment in industry is not a grubby rat race or a last resort if no other employment is available, but a vital and worthwhile element in our modern way of life which also provides opportunities for involvement in sport and the arts.

This particular Conference today is designed to demonstrate that industrial companies are also playing their part in caring for the environment.

Ever since the Industrial Revolution it has been quite evident that thoughtless and unscrupulous industrial development causes serious harm to the natural and human environment. Less than 40 years ago – if there are any of you old enough to remember that – all our major industrial centres were suffering from serious air pollution, and all the rivers which had the misfortune to run anywhere near them had lost every vestige of life at all. Since those days the clean-up has been dramatic and many industrial companies have made valuable contributions to this process.

In 1975 the 3M Company introduced a 3P programme, standing for 'Pollution Prevention Pays'. Reporting on the programme in 1982 the company claimed – and I suspect with a certain amount of surprise – that $100 million had been saved and that about 60 per cent of that total was in operating costs. 3M estimated that to earn the same amount would have required $300 million in additional sales per year, or the equivalent of its annual sales in 1981 alone.

One very interesting point is, of course, the importance of caring in advance. I think that the contribution from the Gas Board was a particularly valuable one, although it was not the only contribution. It is vitally important to think ahead. We have heard about the problems of reclamation, the damage that people have done, and actually the chairman of the last session admitted himself that he did not know what he was doing. There are an awful lot of people about in this world who do not know what they are doing.

Another point that came out concerned the consequences of having a philosophy. The Body Shop contribution was a marvellous example showing that if you start off with a philosophy all sorts of things flow from it.[4] So it is important for people to have the basic idea, the basic concept, and then all sorts of things will flow from it. You cannot really do it the other way round.

17th May 1973.
Address to the Scottish Wildlife Trust.
Glasgow.

One very important and valuable development in recent years has been the determination to clean up and tidy up areas devastated by the early days of the Industrial Revolution. The scale of reclamation of derelict land and derelict waterways, which has been achieved in recent years, has resulted in the slow restoration of natural conditions and populations of wildlife on the fringes of many industrial areas, and with any luck and good management, right in the heart of Glasgow. As these reclamation schemes develop through this heavily populated area of Scotland, these parks and walkways will be an immense advantage to the local people.

There is much talk about the approaching doom of our civilization due to unrestricted population growth, the exhaustion of natural resources currently in demand and the pollution of land, air and water. There are dangers; but disaster isn't around the corner. I think we should look at it from a different point of view. How much better life would be for all of us if we could get rid of pollution, if we could correct some of the mistakes of the past, and if we could achieve a reasonably stable population to allow room for all our needs.

Trade in Wild Species

6th February 1985.
Lecture on Trade in Endangered Species.
Cambridge University.

The exploitation of wild species for export as food or for their products, or alive for collectors and researchers, is taking place on a massive scale. The legal or illegal taking of animals and plants from the wild is done by individuals or by gangs; it is not an organized industry. The consumers, in many instances, are tourists, casual shoppers and individuals who have no reason to know the damaging consequences of their demands.

Just to give you an idea of the scale of this trade, let me quote some figures. In the late 1950s the total world trade in primates taken in the wild involved nearly 200,000 animals, with the USA taking more than all the other importing countries combined. To a great extent thanks to the introduction of controls, the total world trade in live primates is now down to about 30,000. The majority go to researchers and collectors, but there is one rather curious demand for chimpanzees. Apparently on the beaches of Spanish holiday resorts, freelance photographers go about with one of these cuddly creatures, persuading holiday-makers to hold it in their arms as they pose for photographs. The unsuspecting customers probably consider themselves animal lovers; little do they realize that for every one chimp that makes it to the beach for them to hold, at least five have died on the way. This apparently harmless activity is today the most serious threat to the survival of chimps in the wild.

The extent of the trade in wildlife and wildlife products is quite astonishing. According to IUCN experts something like 1,000 tonnes of ivory, representing 9,000 elephants, appear on the market annually. I can well believe it. I was in Bangkok some years ago, helping to raise money for the conservation of nature in Thailand. On the way out to the airport with the Director General of WWF international, we counted no less than 20 shops, within half a mile of the hotel, all selling ivory products.

It hardly needed very acute perception to recognize that only by controlling this trade could such species by given a chance of survival. In principle, if you can reduce demand then supply should also be reduced. Moves to establish an international convention to control trade in wildlife and its products began seriously in 1960 at the IUCN General Assembly in Warsaw. By 1964 the first draft had been prepared by the IUCN and tentative lists of species needing protection drawn up and submitted to governments and international agencies such as FAO (Food and Agriculture Organization) and GATT (General Agreement on Tariffs and Trade). The final draft was agreed in Washington in 1973, and the Convention came into effect on 1st July 1975, ratified by 10 nations. Today there are 87 parties to CITES (Convention on International Trade in Endangered Species) covering the main exporting and importing countries; but there are some serious gaps, particularly in Mexico, Singapore and some of the North African countries. Unfortunately, these loop-holes are assiduously exploited by unscrupulous traders. The only effective way to put them out of business is to remove the demand for their services.

The parties to CITES recognize the 'international co-operation is essential for the protection of certain species of wild flora and fauna against over-exploitation through international trade'. The Convention provides for a world-wide system of controls on trade in wildlife, alive or dead, or in 'readily recognizable parts' of animals and plants.

Protected species are listed in three appendices: Appendix 1 lists species threatened with extinction by trade. Except for strictly scientific purposes, no permit may be issued for international trade in these species. Among those listed are all apes and lemurs, many of the South American monkeys, river dolphins, great whales, cheetah, leopard, snow leopard, clouded leopard, Asiatic lion, tiger, many of the small cats, Asian elephant, rhinos, several deer and wild cattle, many of the birds of prey, cranes, pheasants, *Amazona* parrots, turtles, giant tortoises, crocodiles, monitor lizards, Komodo dragon, Japanese and Chinese giant salamanders, giant catfish, many mussels, and orchids.

Appendix 2 lists species liable to be endangered by trade and which therefore require monitoring 'in order to avoid utilization incompatible with their survival'; but trade is permitted provided it is properly documented. Species listed include all primates, otters, African elephants, fur seals, big-horn sheep, birds of paradise, sturgeons, coelacanth, some snails, bird-wing butterflies, black corals and cacti.

Appendix 3 lists species which individual countries wish to protect for their own reasons, although they may be common elsewhere.

Before any effective controls can be applied it is obviously essential to establish the facts and to keep them up to date. In 1976 the IUCN Species Survival Commission set up the Trade Records Analysis of Fauna and Flora in Commerce, commonly known as TRAFFIC. The head-quarters is here in Cambridge as part of the Wildlife Trade Monitoring Unit and TRAFFIC offices have also been set up in the USA, Germany, Japan, Belgium, the Netherlands and in East Africa, and one is about to open in Australia. Most of these offices are funded by the WWF and each of them publishes information in one form or another. The WTMU (Wildlife Trade Monitoring Unit) publishes 'TRAFFIC Bulletin' which is funded by the PTES.

All parties reserve the right to permit trade in certain listed species. For instance, France, Italy, Japan, and Switzerland have reserved the right to trade in crocodile skins, and, needless to say, Japan has reserved the right to trade in whales. Parties may obviously exercise stricter control than is required under the Convention.

The CITES secretariat is located in Lausanne and acts as a link between the parties, arranges meetings, undertakes scientific and technical studies and lays down standards for preparation and shipment of living specimens and means of identification, and, of course, is closely associated with the WTMU here in Cambridge which provides information and statistics for all the parties.

A system of permits and licences for the movement of listed species has been established using security printing to discourage forgery and misrepresentation. If the price is right, smuggling in any merchandise is inevitable. Some years ago I was in Ethiopia helping to persuade the Emperor to establish a Department of National Parks and Wildlife. With the help of a British adviser, a retired Air Force officer, whose name I remember as Gizzaw, was found and appointed as Head of the Department and we all congratulated ourselves on this achievement. About a year later I got a frantic letter from the British adviser with the news that, as rumours had been circulating that all was not well in the Department, he had decided to inspect its store.

To his horror he found it piled high with fur skins, tusks and wildlife trophies of all sorts. It then transpired that Gizzaw had been running a lucrative black market in wildlife products.

As with all such international conventions, their effectiveness depends on proper enforcement. Governments, particularly of the poorer countries, have the greatest difficulty in setting up efficient management authorities and in training sufficient customs officers to recognize the CITES listed species. Even when some illegal trade is detected the penalties are often insufficient to act as a deterrent. Furthermore, the illegal traders are probably pretty wealthy, and many governments are disinclined to irritate them.

The clue to effective control is an efficient customs service both in the exporting and in the importing countries. The difficulty, of course, is that until CITES came along there was really no reason for customs officers to know one species from another. Inevitably they have to rely on help and advice from Natural History and Zoological societies, but to provide them with immediate reference material CITES has produced a series of identification manuals in loose-leaf form so that they can be made up to suit the requirements of each particular country.

I think it is important to stress here that the reputable trade associations of businesses involved in the processing of wildlife products fully support CITES. They see it as the best insurance for the continuation of their businesses. Without these controls they can see quite clearly that their raw materials are in serious danger of dying out.

One of the great subjects of debate among conservationists is the farming or ranching of wild species, particularly of endangered species. There is nothing wrong with the general principle from the purely conservation point of view. The difficulty is to ensure that unscrupulous farmers and traders don't use the system to mask their exploitation of the species in the wild. The issue is further confused by well-meaning groups who force a boycott on the sale of particular wildlife products on the endangered list, whether farmed or taken from the wild. Such action may seem to them to be the obvious thing to do, but it may well have serious economic consequences for the communities which had been dependent on the taking of the animals from the wild, and which, subsequent to the boycott, must be converted to farming them instead. In some cases, such as that of the Atlantic salmon, it might well be argued that salmon farming has done more to prevent the extinction of the species than anything else.

An alternative, and even more satisfactory solution to the problem of taking animals for their skins is to make the material artificially.

I have already mentioned that CITES has been instrumental in achieving a substantial reduction in the trade in primates. It can also claim a good many other successes. WTMU now stores and processes the data relating to all the trade transactions reported by the parties to the Convention. All imports reported by a particular country are compared with all exports any other party has reported sending to that country, and the same is done for all exports reported. All imports recorded by each country are compared with reports from the countries of origin. In addition all exports and imports of a particular species or group reported by each party are compared. As this process becomes more comprehensive, it will become possible to assess the volume of trade in any CITES species and, by measuring the discrepancies, it will be possible to estimate the effectiveness of the control measures and the extent and location of illegal trade and smuggling.

I have visited a number of TRAFFIC offices in the last couple of years and, judging by the amount of illegal items confiscated by the customs, the system is beginning to work reasonably well. Needless to say, confiscation is not a success in itself. It is too late to save the animals concerned, unless they are still alive; and even then they are lost to the wild population, so they are as good as dead. Success, from the conservation point of view, depends on achieving a decline in poaching and illegal trading; and as yet there is a long way to go before the decline will be sufficient to make a significant contribution to the chances of survival of endangered species. For CITES to work properly it desperately needs the goodwill and support of customs officials, legitimate traders and, above all, the public at large, particularly in the richer nations, the ultimate consumers. If CITES fails to work, I am afraid that many more species will be sharing the same fate as the Dodo.

1st October 1980.
The Fairfield Osborne Lecture.
New York.

I suppose my nearest contact with Fairfield Osborne[5] was in the launching of the United States National Appeal of the World Wildlife Fund in 1962. I was fortunate enough to be able to attend the inaugural dinner here in New

York. It is such a long time ago now that I cannot remember all the details, but I do remember getting into diplomatic hot water for suggesting that a certain country with a vast and rapidly expanding population did not really need the assistance of products of rhinoceros horns for certain natural functions. As it happens the poor rhinos now have another problem to contend with. Their horns are in great demand for the purpose of making the handles of those ceremonial daggers worn with the traditional dress in certain parts of the Arabian peninsula.

It is instances such as these – and there are any number of them – which are liable to turn otherwise calm and sensible conservationists into militant fanatics. This is unfortunate, for two reasons. First, because anger usually makes people rude and insulting; and that is certainly not the way to win friends and influence people. Secondly, anger makes people thrash out blindly in all directions so that, if they actually succeed in making any impression at all, it is more by good luck than good judgement.

In anything to do with conservation, I believe it is particularly important to keep cool, read the World Conservation Strategy, think deeply and be particularly careful to identify the interest of the people and groups most directly involved. It is then a matter of dealing with each situation in the most appropriate and effective way. Uncompromising confrontation may work sometimes but any reasonably intelligent person is more likely to respond to explanation and a well-argued case for conservation.

Exploitation of the Natural System

4th June 1982.
The Chancellor's Lecture, Salford University.

Perhaps the two worst examples of lack of consideration are the demand for pet animals that have to be caught in the wild and the demand for the products of wild animals. The pet trade is having a very serious influence on the chances of survival of a large number of species of birds, mammals and reptiles; and even tortoises are getting scarce. Part of the trouble, of course, is that for every animal finding an owner, as many as half a dozen may die on the way. The demand for articles of clothing or decoration made from animals caught in the wild is probably even more damaging. The furs, particularly of leopards and ocelots, and skins of reptiles such as snakes, crocodiles and caymans, and turtle-shells must be classed as luxuries: they are certainly not essential human needs.

It is the demand for such articles, and the prices people are willing to pay for them, that encourages the whole criminal sequence of poaching, corruption, smuggling and clandestine distribution; and the final irony is that many of these products soon acquire a rarity value, which only makes matters worse. The sad part about it is that, in spite of the prices demanded, most of the buyers of these pets and products are too ignorant, or perhaps too naïve, to appreciate the consequences of their demand; and I am sure they do not appreciate the consequences of their purchases.

Down to Earth

21st September 1982.
Address to the World Affairs Council.
Los Angeles.

At least demands for food and raw materials are understandable; the demand for exotic pets, knick-knacks and luxuries derived from wild populations threatened with extinction is simply irresponsible. The trouble is that tourists and importers are too ignorant or naïve to appreciate what they are doing. Did you know, for example, that last year the United States alone imported 10,000 square metres of elephant skin? Which, I am reliably informed by an enthusiastic researcher, is enough to cover three football fields although he admits that it was probably not used for this purpose. In an average year, 700,000 live birds – half of them parrots – are imported into this country; are there really so many people who see themselves as Long John Silver? 125 million tropical fish; can there be so many psychiatrists' waiting rooms? 500,000 orchids, 10 million cacti, 420,000 live reptiles, plus a million reptile skins. And that is only what is imported into the United States; the lists for Japan and Europe are equally frightening. Just stop to think: where can all this stuff be coming from? The world's wildlife can stand so much exploitation, but irresponsible plunder on this scale can clearly not continue much longer. The point to remember is that if there is a demand, some starving inhabitant of a poor country will provide the supply even if it means catching or killing, legally or illegally, the last remaining animal. The only hope is to remove the demand, and help the poor to survive by other means.

Exploitation of the Natural System

31st May 1984.
Introduction to the Zoological Society of London Symposium.

Just to illustrate the scale of these problems, let me give you some figures on world trade in wildlife and wildlife products which were produced for the meeting of the WWF Council in Washington recently because there was a discussion about this particular subject. And these, I may say, are minimum estimates, and include both legal and illegal trade.

15 million fur skins, plus another 35 million from captive-bred animals.

2.5 million live reptiles, 10 million raw skins and 20 million products.

10 million cacti, 1 million orchids, and of both of those most are taken from the wild.

350 million ornamental fish, mostly tropical, many taken from the wild.

3 million live birds; 0.5 million parrots alone from a relatively small area in South America.

40,000 primates, most of which are used for bio-chemical research.

700,000 kg of raw ivory and 28 million ivory products; and just to remind you, it takes roughly 9 elephants to produce 1,000 kg of ivory, so if you have got a pocket calculator you can figure out what that means.

The total value of all wildlife trade in the United States alone is estimated to be between $800 million and $1 billion annually. And these figures, of course, do not include the value of commercial sea fishing or the number of wild fish taken at sea or in lakes and rivers.

There are signs that the fur trade is also beginning to realize that it is in its interests to support national government legislation designed to conserve the wild species on which their trade depends. I very much hope that other trades and industries, which make use of such natural raw materials, will soon come to the same conclusions. Without such involvement the poachers and the illegal traders will most certainly destroy their trade in the very near future.

15th November 1984.
Speech at a Fund-Raising Dinner of the World Wildlife Fund-UK.
London.

For the moment CITES is not adhered to anything like strictly enough. We can only hope to reduce the taking of endangered species in the wild – nearly always by poachers – if we can control the demand; and the demand comes from the rich and developed nations of this world. Somehow or another we have got to persuade people not to want snakeskin shoes, and turtle or tortoise shell, and leopard-skin coats, and parrots, and tropical fish, and all that sort of thing, because the supply is not endless.

3rd February 1986.
Address to the European Management Forum Foundation Symposium.
Davos.

Forests and plantations provide raw materials for some of the major construction and manufacturing industries, but there are also a number of wild animal populations that provide raw materials for the food–processing industries, such as sea fish; or for the fashion industry, such as skins and furs; and many conventional drugs are derived from wild plants. Traditional medical remedies make use of such things as rhino horn and the less mentionable parts of other animals. This can have a devastating effect on the numbers of the species concerned. For instance, the global rhino population has declined from an estimated 71,000 to 13,000 during the last 15 years.

Because the required species are wild they are considered to be free for all, and even where they are protected by law, it is extremely difficult to enforce the law against determined poachers and illegal traders.

Let me repeat: as far as conservation is concerned, there is nothing wrong with the exploitation of wild species, provided always that it does not threaten the species with extinction. It seems to me, therefore, that all the industries that depend on wild species for their raw materials should be concerned to ensure the security of future supplies. The only way for them to do this is to work together with conservation organizations to preserve the habitats and the well-being of the populations on which their livelihood depends.

20th March 1986.
Speech at the Launch of the World Wildlife Fund-UK's 'Planet Protection '86'.
London.

One of the most destructive human activities is poaching economically valuable wild species. Needless to say, the rarer the species the higher the value. WWF, together with IUCN, was instrumental in setting up the Convention on International Trade in Endangered Species (CITES), and in paying for a system of TRAFFIC offices to monitor the trade. The object is to try to reduce the demand for these endangered species and their products by making it illegal to export them from their home countries and to import them into other countries. Sadly, the demand comes largely from the affluent countries and is an unfortunate reflection on the general ignorance of conservation issues among otherwise well-educated people. This is a good example of the importance of creating awareness.

Commercial Fishing

26th February 1977.
Speech at a Dinner of the World Wildlife Fund.
Wellington, New Zealand.

Some wild populations, once their habitat is made secure, can be left to regulate themselves. Most bird populations come under this category, except, of course, those birds which have decided to share certain agricultural crops with the farmers. Other wild populations, notably fish and whales, have a commercial and nutritional value to man. Some people might like to see them preserved from any form of exploitation but, from the conservation point of view, all that is needed is to ensure that a viable population continues to exist. It is theoretically quite possible to establish a maximum sustainable yield for such populations which will not endanger the species as a whole. This has been tried by the International Whaling Commission, but if certain governments simply ignore the rules it is virtually impossible to do anything about it – short of sinking their whale catchers and factory ships.

1st October 1980.
The Fairfield Osborne Lecture.
New York.

The International Whaling Commission, which controls the Convention agreed by the whaling industries, introduced a series of catch quotas for each species based on an estimate of their maximum sustainable yield, and, in addition, the largest species, the blue whale, the humpback and the Pacific grey whale, were given complete protection from whaling by factory ships. The most recent steps were taken in 1979 when only minke whales were allowed to be taken by factory ships and the Indian Ocean Whale Sanctuary was declared. This is the largest sanctuary ever created for any animal group and includes the whole Indian Ocean down to latitude 55°S. Altogether not an inconsiderable achievement.

9th March 1983.
Speech to the Vancouver Canadian Club.

On the way here we sailed up the coast of Lower California where the grey whales breed. When commercial whaling started on the American West Coast in 1851 it is estimated that some 50,000 grey whales migrated along the coast to and from the Arctic Seas. Twenty years later barely 8,000 were still making the journey.

Captain Scammon, a whaling captain, published a book in 1874 on the Marine Animals of the North Coast of North America.

Writing about the grey whale he says:

> *'The mammoth bones of the California Grey lie bleaching on the shores of those silvery waters, and are scattered along the broken coasts, from Siberia to the Gulf of California; and ere long it may be questioned whether this mammal will not be numbered among the extinct species of the Pacific.'*

Fortunately his fears were not realized and now, thanks to complete protection, the population has recovered to an estimated 18,000. We were lucky enough to see a number of them in one of their winter resort lagoons, before the start of the migration north.

4th June 1982.
The Chancellor's Lecture, Salford University.

I am sure you have all heard of the great whaling controversy involving the Japanese and Russian whaling fleets. Whaling is supposed to be controlled by the International Whaling Commission on the basis of maintaining viable and stable populations, but the great difficulty is to arrive at generally acceptable figures for whale populations. Not unnaturally the whaling nations draw the most optimistic conclusions from their own figures while the Commission's scientific advisers tend to draw the most pessimistic conclusions from their figures. The latest news is that Japan is intending to take up to 400 sperm whales a year for the next two years in spite of a total ban imposed by the IWC. Japan has also announced that it will take 3,027 minke whales and, in a splendid example of 'one-upmanship', the Soviet Union has announced that it will take 3,028 minke whales this year, in spite of a total IWC quota of 3,900.

The problem for Japan is that whale meat is seen as a traditional part of the diet and, of course, there is always the political argument that any restriction on the whaling industry will put people out of work. Furthermore, the Japanese seem to be convinced that the campaign to restrict whaling is entirely motivated by prejudice against their way of life and particularly their eating habits.

I have spoken to two Prime Ministers of Japan in recent

years trying to convince them that proper conservation of whale stocks will ensure that the Japanese will continue to be able to enjoy whale meat whereas the present rate of exploitation is very likely to result in the extinction of a number of whale species.

6th February 1985.
Lecture on Trade in Endangered Species.
Cambridge University.

Progress in the development of commercial sea-fishing techniques has had a really serious impact on fish stocks. Conservation measures are now being taken but not before the North Sea fishermen have virtually put themselves out of business. The World Conservation Strategy points out that as a direct result of over-fishing the current world catch is some 20 per cent lower today than it might have been. Continued technical improvements to the perform-ance of the fishing boats, the introduction of electronic detection devices, monofilament nets and more powerful winches, have made herring fishing much more efficient, whilst the French predilection for herring roe, needless to say, did nothing to encourage the replacement of stocks. All these factors together had the entirely predictable and predicted result that all herring fishing in the North Sea had to be banned for several years to allow the stocks to recover.

Much the same thing is happening to the Atlantic salmon, and unless some drastic measures are taken fairly soon it will be another species in danger of extinction. The trouble is, of course, that fishing in the oceans is free for all and this means that it is not in the interest of any of the fishing fleets to control the exploitation since they each know that if they don't catch the last remaining fish one of their competitors will certainly do so.

The collapse of the herring population came about in Europe in spite of the relative prosperity of the countries involved; in spite of the strength of their conservation movements, and in spite of the existence of the EEC. That gives you some idea of how much more difficult it is to control over-exploitation of commercially valuable wild resources in less well-organized and poorer parts of the world. A few years ago, the waters around Iceland beyond the three-mile territorial waters limit were free-for-all, and the consequent over-fishing reduced the stocks of fish to a dangerously low level. Then, after a considerable struggle – the two so-called 'Cod Wars' – Iceland succeeded in gaining proprietorial fishing rights out to 200 miles, and it is now in a position to conserve the fish stocks in that area. In effect, Iceland now farms those waters which used to be free-for-all and were consequently exploited without restraint.

1st October 1980.
The Fairfield Osborne Lecture.
New York.

The whole of the North Sea was thrown open to the fishermen of all the members of the EEC just at the time when fishing techniques were becoming increasingly efficient. In consequence it was over-fished and there is now a severe restriction on the taking of most species of fish and much unemployment among fishermen. In effect no country has any proprietary rights, and therefore there is no inducement for the fishermen to conserve fish stocks. And, apart from the EEC itself, there is no fishing organization to which the fishermen can belong which has the purpose of administering a conservation policy in their interests.

18th February 1981.
Address to the All-Party Conservation Committee.
London.

The trouble is that the fishermen cannot very well be blamed because outside the old three-mile limit fishing was free-for-all, and without internationally observed catch limits, fishermen knew that if they did not catch the last fish someone else would. Perhaps the most dangerous development has been the virtual 'vacuum cleaning' method of fishing where everything caught is immediately converted into fish-meal for domestic animal feed or fertilizer. It is to deal with all these problems that the World Wildlife Fund has launched the 'Seas Must Live' campaign.

4th June 1982.
The Chancellor's Lecture, Salford University.

In recent years we have seen a total ban on the fishing for herring in the North Sea. The wild population of herring which, not many years ago, must have numbered untold millions, was so seriously over-exploited by commercial fishing that the herring, if not in danger of total extinction, could have reached a point where its recovery might have been in doubt. Properly managed, there could be a very considerable sustainable yield of herring for years to come. Unfortunately there is no evidence that this lesson has been learned and today the rate at which mackerel are being taken around our coasts cannot possibly be sustained for very much longer. And to make matters worse, the nursery areas for many species of edible fish are found in tidal estuaries and shallow coastal waters, areas most prone to reclamation and so-called coast defence works.

A classic example of the international nature of the problem of conservation is the Atlantic salmon. Spawned in the rivers of North America and Western Europe, success depending on the degree of river pollution, including the effects of acid rain, it migrates to feed and grow in the sub-arctic waters around Greenland, north of Iceland and Spitzbergen. It is fished in these areas and again on its way back to breed. It is netted off river mouths and finally fished in its home rivers before spawning. The problem of applying and enforcing adequate conservation measures in such a case is extremely complex. And a further factor is that river authorities are unlikely to continue to operate hatcheries merely to see their products taken in the sea far from home.

III

THE POPULATION
FACTOR

Population, or the number of individual members of a particular species, is a crucial factor in the whole natural system. Too few, and the species is in danger of becoming extinct; too many, and the species is liable to damage its own habitat and to threaten the survival of other species. Like everything to do with the world's natural system, the population factor is dynamic. All the elements in the inter-relationship between species are in a constant state of flux. Even without human interference there would be successes and disasters, and the equilibrium of the natural system would fluctuate from year to year.

What has been described as the 'balance of nature' is simply nature's system of self-limitation. Fertility and breeding success create the surpluses after allowing for the replacement of losses. Predation, climatic variation, disease and starvation – and in the case of the inappropriately named *Homo sapiens*, wars and terrorism – are the principal means by which population numbers are kept under some sort of control.

Viewed dispassionately, it must be obvious that the world's human population has grown to such a size that it is threatening its own habitat; and it has already succeeded in causing the extinction of large numbers of wild plant and animal species. Some have simply been killed off. Others have quietly disappeared as their habitats have been taken over or disturbed by human activities.

The important point is that human interference with the

natural system has created an entirely new situation. It is far too late to try to preserve the natural system as it existed two hundred years ago. That is gone for ever. What we can do is to try to protect and manage the most valuable, in terms of species diversity, of the few remaining natural habitats and wilderness areas. Above all, we must use every possible means to prevent the extinction of wild species.

The Human Population Explosion

11th March 1987.
Address to the Joint Meeting of the Joint Group on Population and
Development and the All-Party Conservation Committee.
London.

To make any comment about human population is just about as dangerous as going for a Sunday afternoon walk in a mine-field. I do believe, however, that human population pressure – the sheer number of people on this planet – is the single most important cause of the degradation of the natural environment, of the progressive extinction of wild species of plants and animals, and of the destabilization of the world's climatic and atmospheric systems.

The problem about even so much as mentioning the subject of the world's human population is that people immediately jump to the conclusion that you are going to talk about the shocking subjects of population control and family planning. As these seem to have a Pavlovian effect on some people, and are anyway specialized subjects, I want to make it clear that I have no intention of stepping on those particular mines. All I want to do is to draw your objective attention to the influence which human population growth has had, and continues to have, on the rest of the world's plant and animal life, as well as on the whole natural system, which sustains all life on this planet.

I expect most of you know the basic facts (I mean the

population facts, not the facts of life). In round figures, the present world population of the species *Homo sapiens* is 5,000 million, and it is expected to grow to 6 billion by the year 2000. Two hundred years ago the figure was about 1,000 million, and it does not require a great stretch of the imagination to appreciate that with a population of that size the pressure on natural resources and the degradation of the natural environment would be very much less.

Population dynamics is a very complicated subject, but assuming that the present slowing down of the rate of growth continues – and the economists do not win the argument for continued growth – it looks as if numbers should eventually stabilize at about 10 billion sometime in the next century.

To put that in perspective: the simple fact is that the world's human population has quadrupled in the last two hundred years. Or, to put it another way, the population of China today – about 1 billion – is a bit more than that of the population of the whole world two hundred years ago.

It is easy enough to generalize about the problems caused by population growth, but I thought it might bring the points home more forcefully if I chose a particular case as an example.

The following facts about Kenya are derived from a pamphlet called *The Shape of Things to Come* produced by Population Concern a few years ago.

At the moment Kenya has the world's fastest growing population. It is running at about 4 per cent per annum. This means that its 1980 population of 16 million will double in the next eighteen years. If present trends continue, this will mean an increase in the urban population of over 300 per cent, and an increase in the labour force of

96 per cent – from 5 million in 1975 to 10.2 million in the year 2000. By that year the education system will have to cope with an extra 2.3 million children and the number of hospital beds will have to go up from about 17,000 to over 100,000. You can imagine the economic problems the government will have to face in providing adequate water supplies, food, housing and employment on such a scale. I hope you can also imagine the effect it will have on the natural environment. This is a particularly serious consideration for Kenya since it derives so much economic benefit from tourists attracted by its magnificent National Parks and wildlife.

To quote from the pamphlet:

> '*Per capita agricultural output has been declining since 1972 as this growth (in the population) has forced people into farming marginal lands and, at the same time, caused the deterioration of the better lands.*
>
> *Moreover, Kenya presents a challenge to the classic "demographic transition" theory which claims that a reduction in a country's fertility rate is automatically achieved by the spread of education, improved health and lower mortality and new economic expectation . . .*
>
> *Ironically Kenya's success in social and economic development has helped push up the rate of population growth.*'

There are, of course, a number of countries such as Fiji, Barbados and Thailand, which have been successful in controlling their population growth by voluntary means, and consequently do not face the same daunting problems as Kenya, but they are the exceptions.

Incidentally, a statistician told me yesterday that the rate of growth of the GNP of Japan and Brazil had been the same since the war. The only difference between them was the growth of the Brazilian population.

The Deputy Prime Minister of Fiji speaking in Australia last year pointed out:

> *'In the 1960s we were able to significantly reduce our rate of population growth through family planning.*
>
> *Clearly at a time of adverse economic conditions and rising unemployment we would have now been facing a disastrous situation. We have therefore re-emphasised the importance of management of the rate of increase of our population in our development strategy for the next five years. This is not only to ensure that growth per capita income is not eroded by rapid population increase, but also to control the inflow into our labour force in line with our capacity to create jobs.'*

I have quoted the situation in Kenya because it illustrates a number of points in the relationship between population and the conservation of nature.

First of all, urban growth. The concentration of large populations means that the pressure on the surrounding land to produce the food and fuel requirements virtually denies it to any other form of life. Furthermore these huge cities generate an immense demand for clean water and fuel-wood, and at the same time they create vast quantities of waste and noxious effluents which pollute the air, and everything downwind, the waters, and everything downstream.

That is the local picture; now look at the global situation. The combined effects of the world's huge conurbations hardly need to be emphasized. It is estimated that by the year 2000 Mexico City will have some 31 million inhabitants, Sao Paulo – 25.8, and Shanghai – 22.7. We can barely cope with the problems of London with a population of only about 9 million.

The social problems alone in these mega-cities are going

to be bad enough, but just imagine what their demands for resources and their effluents will do to the natural environment. As it is the air pollution over these cities has to be seen to be believed.

The next point is the human intrusion into marginal lands. In most cases marginal lands are either scrub, forest or marshland. They are therefore particularly sensitive to change of use and they are also the only areas left to the wild populations of plants and animals. Many of these are known to be valuable to man, many more are potentially valuable.

Marginal lands are important for both native and migratory species and many tidal wetlands and mangrove swamps along coasts are important breeding areas for economically valuable fish. All this is being destroyed in the hope of providing an economic existence for the excess human population. It seldom works for long.

Two years ago I visited some of the countries on the southern border of the Sahara. I discovered that during the fifteen years of more or less drought conditions, the human population had increased by a third, and as the human population increased so the domestic animal population increased with it. The consequence has been the progressive destruction of the natural pastures. What little tree cover once existed has also disappeared as the demand for fuel-wood has increased. In some areas the desert is presently advancing at the rate of six kilometres a year. This is forcing the people of these areas to move south, adding ethnic problems and still more people to the overcrowding in those already swollen populations.

Incidentally, while the world's response with food aid to the famine in that area was most impressive, it seems to have been overlooked that food alone is not much use if there is nothing with which to cook it.

A number of those countries are dependent on the waters of the two great rivers, the Niger and the Senegal, which loop up from the coastal mountains in the south, and flow through the arid central areas before spilling into the Atlantic on the West Coast. The rivers used to be fed by monsoon rains falling on the tropical forests. These forests have now been exploited as a natural economic resource and the denuded soil is silting up the rivers. Furthermore the absence of tree cover on the mountains is said to be having an unsettling effect on the pattern of monsoon rains.

Tropical forests are being exploited all over the world to meet increasing demands, but as they disappear their populations of wild plants and animals disappear with them. India has lost half its tree cover in the last forty years. The FAO predict that Brazil will lose 63 million acres – an area two and a half times the size of Portugal – by the year 2000. All but three per cent of its Atlantic rain forest has already disappeared.

The simple fact is that the human population of the world is consuming natural renewable resources faster than it can regenerate, and the process of exploitation itself is causing even further damage. If this is already happening with a population of 4 billion, I ask you to imagine what things will be like when the population reaches 6 and then 10 billion people

The more people there are on this earth, the more space and resources they need: and the more prosperous they become, the more resources each individual wants. All this has been made possible by the Industrial Revolution and the scientific explosion and it is spread around the world by the new economic religion of development. We have taken it for granted for too long that nature can survive the onslaught of a human population explosion and its growing demands for diminishing resources. If such a thing happened to an animal population, it would soon suffer a catastrophic collapse, as its habitat became degraded and unable to support such a large population.

It has also happened to human populations in the past. If you look around the globe you will find that most of the deserts are man-made. The populations of ancient civilizations grew in numbers until their resources became exhausted, and they faded into extinction, with only a few ruins to mark their folly. The difference this time is that it is a global civilization and we are using up global, instead of local resources.

The sad thing is that it is all done with the very best intentions. But good intentions do not justify major environmental and social disasters, nor the gradual destruction of the only planet we have for our existence and for the existence of the generations who, we hope, will follow us.

We should be looking at the natural living world, which shares this planet with us, in the same way that the miners used to look at their canaries. They knew that if the canary died it would be their turn next, unless they acted very quickly indeed.

The mass of the world's human population is suffocating its canary. There is still enough life in it to be saved, if we act quickly. If we let it die we will be condemning future generations to experience an increasingly rapid decline of the natural system on which their life depends.

Much as we all deplore the existence of nuclear weapons, nuclear war is still only a possibility. The degradation of the natural environment is an actuality. Like a child blowing up a balloon, everything looks perfectly normal right up to the instant that the balloon explodes. I cannot help wondering how much more the world's natural system can stand before it suddenly collapses.

I can tell you what effect the human population is having on the natural world and the natural system, but I cannot tell you what we should be doing about the human population numbers. That is up to people like yourselves, who have volunteered to take the awkward social and political decisions. You have not got much time, so for the sake of future generations, I hope you get them right.

What started out as concern for wildlife has rapidly become concern for human life. While it is not exactly easy to make the survival of wildlife much more than an abstract concept for most people, it is relatively simple to get people to be concerned about the quality of their own survival.

16th July 1973.
Address at the Salford University Degree Ceremony.

There may be disagreements about the time scale, but in principle there can be little doubt that the population cannot go on increasing indefinitely. Resources presently being used will not last for ever and pollution in its broadest sense, unless severely checked, is bound to increase with population and industrial activity.

The real discussion begins with the problem of how to react to this situation and what, if anything, can and should be done about it. The idea of population control, when man has spent thousands of years trying to survive, is a concept which many people find almost impossible to comprehend. Even if it is comprehended, the practical difficulties it entails are so daunting that it is not surprising that so many people shrug their shoulders and escape the issue by saying 'something will happen'. The trouble is that things have 'happened' before, which effectively limited or reduced populations, and they have always been extremely unpleasant for those who experienced them. I cannot really imagine anyone in this day and age advocating famine, pestilence or war as satisfactory methods of population control.

18th February 1981.
Address to the All-Party Conservation Committee.
London.

I suspect that the single most important gift of progress to conservation has been the development of human contraception techniques. The natural world is at greater risk from the *Homo sapiens* population explosion than from any other cause. Not just in terms of the numbers, although they alone are significant simply because of the area occupied – and polluted – by people. Even more important is their growing demand for food and for the products of every kind of animal and plant as well as for non-renewable resources.

The World Wildlife Fund and the International Union for the Conservation of Nature are trying to control the worst excesses by getting countries to sign the Convention on International Trade in Endangered Species.

I hope the day will come when these two organizations combine with the family planning groups to step up the campaign for voluntary population limitation before lack of food and resources makes it compulsory.

This is a classic case of a conflict of interest between individual parents, who naturally feel entitled to have as many children as they please, and the world at large which patently will not be able to support a natural world as well as to feed and house a vastly inflated human population.

1st October 1980.
The Fairfield Osborne Lecture.
New York.

As Fairfield Osborne saw so clearly, the greatest threat to the future of the earth is the unchecked human population explosion. It seemed at that time that 'man', and presumably 'woman' in this case, was being guilty of gross irresponsibility. That obviously is not true because a great many parents are highly responsible and furthermore, fortunately perhaps, there are a great many people who have no children at all. The trouble is that there are so many females of breeding age who are either ignorant or irresponsible, or sometimes both ignorant and irresponsible, and so many men to encourage them to be irresponsible. Before anyone jumps to conclusions, let me say at once that I am not discussing the morality of contraception, I am merely drawing attention to the obvious fact that if only 90 per cent of all female children born alive, live to breeding age, and go on to have more than two or three children each, it automatically feeds the population explosion.

The Population Factor

4th June 1982.
The Chancellor's Lecture, Salford University.

Even though there are now many more single parent families and there are such things as test-tube babies, the normal, perhaps I should say, the traditional system by which children are produced involves two people. As long ago as 1798 Malthus explained what happens when the factors limiting the increase in any population are removed. One of the factors noticed by Darwin was that all species are capable of producing vastly greater populations than can be sustained by existing resources. The observation that in a normal state of balance populations did not increase at the rate at which they are capable of increasing was the basis for his theory of Evolution by Natural Selection.

A. R. Wallace, who came to much the same conclusion as Darwin, put the point this way.

> *'Very few birds produce fewer than two young ones each year while many have six, eight or ten. Four will certainly be below the average and if we suppose that each pair produces only four times in their life, that will also be below average. A simple calculation will show that in fifteen years each pair of birds would have increased to nearly ten million. As on the lowest calculation the progeny are each year twice as numerous as their parents, it follows that whatever be the average number of individuals existing in any given country, twice that number must perish annually.'*

The relevance to natural selection of this capacity for over-production is that as each individual is slightly different to all the others it is probable that under natural conditions those individuals which happen to be best adapted to the prevailing circumstances have a better chance of survival.

149

Well, so what? Well, take a look at the figures for the human population of this world. One hundred and fifty years ago it stood at about 1,000 million or in common parlance today, 1 billion. It then took about a hundred years to double to 2 billion. It took thirty years to add the third billion and fifteen years to reach today's total of 4.4 billion. With a present world average rate of growth of 1.8 per cent the total population by the year 2000 will have increased to an estimated 6 billion and in that and in subsequent years a hundred million people will be added to the world population each year. In fact it could be as much as 16 billion by 2045. As a consequence the demand on resources of land alone will mean a third less farm land available and the destruction of half the present area of productive tropical forest. Bearing in mind the constant reduction of non-renewable resources, there is a strong possibility of growing scarcity and reduction of standards. More people consume more resources. It is as simple as that; and transferring resources and standards from the richer to the poorer countries can only have a marginal effect in the face of this massive increase in the world population.

Meanwhile the more people there are on this earth, the less room there will be for any other species. Domestic animals will have to be husbanded even more intensively than they are at present. Wild species traditionally harvested by man, such as fish, will be put under intolerable pressure by the increase in demand, and the non-useful wild species will find it more and more difficult to exist at all.

The Population Factor

14th December 1983.
Speech at the Margaret Pyke Memorial Trust Dinner.
London.

Fifteen years ago I was very pleased to be invited to open the Margaret Pyke Centre.[1] I may say that I accepted the invitation with a certain amount of trepidation as in those days the mere mention of family planning or birth control was greeted by the media with a 'shock horror' reaction as if these hardened writers had been brought up in a convent. In fact I suspect the only reason the BBC was going to be here was because the words 'birth control' were mentioned. Well a lot of things may have got worse in the intervening years but at least more people seem to have learned the facts of life and to recognize that family planning and birth control are important and sensible subjects for discussion, even if there are still differences of opinion about them.

I believe that this is a development of major importance because so long as they remained taboo subjects the chances of making any impression on the human population explosion were that much more remote.

I have no intention of going into the facts of the population explosion this evening. If anyone present is still unaware of the fact that the total human population of the world is now some 4,500 million and increasing, I am told, at the rate of 1 million every five days, I can only remind you of the quotation from Swift: 'There's none so blind as they that will not see.'

The consequences of this vast increase in population should also be patently evident for all to understand, even if they have not actually seen the shanty towns and slums of the rapidly growing cities of Latin America, Africa and Asia. Mexico City had a population of about 5 million in 1960, it is now 15 million and is expected to reach 28 million by the year 2000. I was in Mexico City in 1960 and you could hardly move then. The pollution was something appalling, so what on earth it's going to be like in the year 2000 I shudder to think.

I was in Bombay recently, where the population has nearly doubled in the last twenty years. If you fly into Bombay, the shanty areas are only too obvious from the air, and from the ground for that matter. It is quite unreasonable to expect any local authority to provide building land, houses, water, sewage, waste disposal, schools and hospitals or to expect that adequate employment will be found for the flood of migrants.

I am President of World Wildlife Fund International and also Vice-President of the International Union for Conservation of Nature and Natural Resources. Both these organizations are trying to cope with the consequences for the natural environment of the human population explosion. Or to put it crudely, the more room taken up and the more resources demanded by the human species, the less room and the fewer resources are left for the wild species of animals and plants.

In the introduction to the IUCN Red Data Books which list all animals and plants under threat of extinction it says that virtually everywhere the major threat to wild species is loss of habitat to a rapidly increasing human population requiring more space in order to build villages and cities and grow more food. But starvation and poverty cannot be eradicated solely by increased food and resources at the expense of what remains of the natural world. Any increase in the provision of food and resources must be accompanied by a drastic reduction in the rate of increase in the human population.

The population explosion is the single most important cause of degradation of the human environment and quality of life as well as the major cause of the destruction of the natural environment and extinction of species. I think it is the realization of this fact that has brought family planners and those concerned with human and natural environments together in Common Ground International.[2]

Only through such co-operation will it ever be possible to gain an understanding of the attitudes and inhibitions of various groups in society to family planning, and from there to develop appropriate and integrated education by means of public awareness campaigns. This is essential for the very good reason that awareness and acceptance are vital preconditions for effective action. And incidentally, awareness can come about in unexpected ways. For instance, a campaign was recently launched in India to improve the quality of cattle for both dairy and draught purposes. It was soon discovered that the process of explaining modern methods of cattle breeding to villagers very quickly triggered off enquiries about human breeding, which in turn enabled family planning methods to be discussed and used.

Much as we should welcome the increasing knowledge and understanding of the population explosion and the growing willingness of people and governments to take family planning and birth control seriously, we are still left with the most intractable problem of all. How to persuade the hundred of millions of actual and potential, rich and poor parents all over the world to limit the size of their families; and how to explain to them how to do it. Various methods are being tried, ranging from the activities of the voluntary bodies such as the Family Planning Association, Population Concern and the International Planned Parenthood Federation, through to the efforts of International and United News Agencies, and government, economic and social programmes.

There is evidence that all these activities are beginning to have an effect on the overall figure, but the dramatic drop in population growth in some areas is unfortunately counter-balanced by persistently high rates of increase in others. The fact is that success has been achieved in the areas of least resistance and greatest understanding; and I believe that from now on the campaign is likely to become increasingly difficult. The very people who are, quite innocently and unknowingly, causing the greatest problem are the ones with whom it is more difficult to communicate.

So, let me just say this to our partners in Common Ground. You can be fully assured of the whole-hearted and active support of every person and organization involved in the conservation of wildlife and natural resources in the campaign to bring the human population explosion under control.

1st July 1983.
Address of Receiving Honorary Degree from the University of Western Ontario. Canada.

Ever since the beginning of human history, the population of every successful community has increased in size and consequently the demand for resources has increased in proportion. Before the arrival of the mechanical age – ushered in as you all know by intelligent industrial revolutionaries – the basic raw material in all classical civilizations was wood. It served as both fuel and building material, and as soon as the forests began to be felled at a faster rate than they could naturally regenerate, the fate of that civilization was sealed.

Just look around the world today and you will notice that the areas once occupied by the Hittites in Asia Minor, the Mesopotamian, Indus and Persian empires are virtual deserts. The ancient civilizations of South East Asia and Central America probably suffered the same fate before they were abandoned and eventually reclaimed by the jungles.

The Industrial Revolution started a new wave of population expansion, thanks to the better farming methods and more efficient techniques for the extraction and processing of mineral and non-renewable resources from the earth and for their manufacture into capital and consumer products. The Industrial Revolution sparked the scientific revolution and brought in its wake better public hygiene, better medical care and yet more efficient agriculture. The consequence was a population explosion which still continues today.

As the population grew, thanks to the very best intentions of highly intelligent scientists and doctors, so the demand for resources and the need for yet more human food became imperative. Measures to improve public health were conspicuously successful. For example, the World Health Organization Project, designed to eradicate malaria in Sri Lanka in the post-war years, achieved its purpose. But the problem today is that Sri Lanka must feed three times the number of mouths, find three times the number of jobs, provide three times the housing, energy, schools, hospitals and land for settlement merely in order to maintain the same standards. Little wonder the natural environment and wildlife in Sri Lanka has suffered. The fact that the best-intentioned aid programmes are at least partially responsible for the problems is all the more reason for intelligent aid programmes to help to solve them.

In India, the population increased in 1982 alone by about 15 million people. The population in 1975 was 607 million. It is expected to be 950 million, or to have increased by 56 per cent, by the year 2000. This means that the labour force will increase by 62 per cent. In order to achieve the same standard of health care as in 1975, the number of physicians must increase by 419 per cent by the year 2000. The number of hospital beds will have to go up from 340,000 to 4.5 million. And that is just an example of the 'Shape of Things to Come', as the publication by Population Concern is aptly titled.

Is all this to do with human greed? Is it greedy to try to provide the food and resources for this growing population inevitably doomed to poverty and deprivation? Does it not have more to do with the intelligence of scientists, agriculturalists, and the best intentions of doctors and international agencies and perhaps the folly of governments and the ignorance of parents?

25th November 1964.
Address at the Freedom from Hunger Campaign's Youth Conference and Progress Report Meeting.
London.

I hope you had a good lunch. I don't think there's anything wrong in that as long as all of us realize that we belong to that fortunate half of the world's population which gets an adequate and a balanced diet. The problem which we have to worry about, and which I hope you are worrying about today, is the other half, which doesn't get enough to eat, or must make do with an inadequate variety of food.

Before we can start doing anything about this problem, it is just as well to know why so many people are in this somewhat unfortunate condition. Since the beginning of time, every population, human, plant, insect or animal, has been controlled in size by the amount of food which it has available. Even as recently as just before the War there were famines in India and in other parts of the world, which carried off millions of people. Next to famine, disease is the great scourge. In recent years both outright famine and a good many of the destructive diseases have been brought under control, and the net result has been what we might expect: an enormous and growing increase in the world population. It has now reached some three thousand million people, and at the present rate of increase, it should more than double that by the year 2000, which, barring accidents, should be with us, or some of us in just over 35 years' time. If you're seventeen now, and my arithmetic is roughly right, you'll be about fifty-two then, and sharing the globe with some six thousand million other people.

I know it may be a glimpse of the obvious, but it is worth remembering that whatever happens to the world population, the globe we live on is most unlikely to get any bigger. To feed this vast population adequately calls for an increase of some 200 per cent in the present production of food.

I suppose one could argue that as starvation has always controlled population there is nothing to worry about. Just let nature take its course. I don't believe any decent human being, least of all a Christian, could possibly accept this argument. No matter how hopeless it may seem, we can't give up without a struggle. We make so many wild claims for ourselves as human beings with a superior intelligence, that I think the least we can do is to prove our superior intelligence by controlling our numbers and standard of existence, deliberately and willingly. We know of nature's solution, but I can't help feeling that we ought to try and do better than that. What's more, we can do better, if we set our minds to it.

This Freedom from Hunger campaign is a start in the right direction. This is not another handout, this is a deliberate and calculated attempt to strike at the root cause of under-nutrition and malnutrition. This is the first comprehensive co-ordinated attempt on a world scale to help people to feed themselves adequately. The idea is to try to break the vicious circle of malnutrition, lethargy, ignorance and starvation, by attacking ignorance: to provide knowledge of food requirements for children, knowledge of better farming methods, knowledge of co-operative marketing organization. This knowledge will surely break this circle, but will require money and technical help applied with understanding, and with enlightenment.

It is important to remember that there is a limit to the exploitation of wild populations. For instance it seemed as if there were any number of whales in the oceans, but already they have been fished out in many areas, and the great blue whale of the Antarctic is on the verge of extinction. Unless wild populations are farmed intelligently, we shall lose one after the other, as a source of food, and incidentally as a source of interest and enjoyment. There is a limit also to what the soil will stand. Erosion and dust bowl farming, or the destruction of vegetation by uncontrolled numbers of domestic animals, can lose more acres in a year than can be gained by all the expensive irrigation and reclamation schemes put together. It is perfectly true that we only cultivate about 8 per cent of the world's land surface. We could increase this to about 30 per cent, but where then would the wild creatures live? The rest of the land surface is either too arid, too mountainous or too cold to cultivate; and of course by the same token, it is not much use to wildlife either.

The Freedom from Hunger campaign can achieve great things, in fact, it's already made a most important impact. But this is only half the solution. Unless we begin to cope with the population explosion, all these achievements will be swallowed up in the flood of humanity. These problems are bad enough now. But it is a pretty safe prediction that unless we mount a massive offensive against them, they will be a great deal more serious by the time your generation is in charge. This is a problem of people, and although we are all equal in the sight of God, the people of the world vary very greatly in their characteristics. We don't all have the same talents and ambitions. We don't all have the same scale of values, and although it may not sound very important, we don't all have the same taste in food. There are lazy, stubborn, dishonest, drunken and generally anti-social people to be found in roughly the same proportion in every part of the world. Somehow or other this great struggling squabbling mass has got to come to realize the gravity of the situation which is confronting it. And it has got to generate the will to do something about it. Make no mistake, for the first time in man's history, we have the power to control our environment and our numbers deliberately. Nature might still have some surprises in store for us, but by and large, if the world runs into a disaster we have only ourselves to blame, for we could have prevented it.

The picture we should keep in our minds is of a world where mankind shares this globe willingly with all God's creatures, where no one is inevitably poor or hungry, and where it is still possible to enjoy a variety of work. This can be achieved, but we must all start working for it now.

I have no doubt that this campaign has its limitations and mistakes. It would be too much to hope that none of the money has been misspent; some useful areas of operation have probably been missed altogether. However, in the broad context of this world problem, the Freedom from Hunger Campaign has been a dazzling success. It has made a tremendous contribution to the solution of the problem of hunger and malnutrition. Even more important, it has pointed the way to further world co-operation, and this is by far the most heartening event to have occurred in our time.

Aid

27th June 1962.
*Launching Address on the Freedom from Hunger Campaign in
the United Kingdom.*
London.

The problems which the Freedom from Hunger Campaign is trying to tackle can be stated quite simply:

First, between 10 and 15 percent of the world's population – some 300 million people – are living at starvation level. They are existing under a permanent threat of death from lack of food.

Second, between 30 and 50 per cent of the world's population – about 1,200 million people – are suffering from malnutrition. In plain words this means that they are getting the wrong sort of diet, which prevents them from developing properly either physically or mentally and which makes them prone to various diseases and general bad health. What's more, it saps the normal human desire to improve the situation.

Somehow we have got to break this vicious circle. The urgency of these problems is very clearly illustrated by the fact that the world's population is expected to increase from just under 3,000 million in 1950 to just over 6,000 million in the year 2000. It may sound as if we had plenty of time, but let me remind you that we shall reach the year 2000 in thirty-eight years' time, within the expected life span of a good many people here today.

I don't recommend looking much further into the future

– somebody worked out the depressing prospect that there would be standing room only in 400 years' time.

Naturally this staggering increase can only take place provided the production of food can keep pace with this growth, otherwise, everything else being equal, we can look forward to the world's population being limited by starvation even more than it is today. Sir John Russell, in the preface to a report by the British Association on Hunger, refers to 'the catastrophic suffering inevitable if world population should outstrip man's power of producing food'. He goes on to say that 'the broad conclusion was that hunger need not be feared for at least the next 40 years and that this result could be achieved on present knowledge if only it were properly applied'.

'At least 40 years' – that may comfort those who don't expect to last that long but it is hardly the sort of thing to make the younger generation wildly enthusiastic about the future.

Statistics can make it look as if food production is in fact keeping ahead of population increase but they ignore two factors. In the first place, the main increase in food production is taking place in Europe and Russia, North America and Australasia, areas which have a high standard of living already. Whereas in many regions where the population is on a low diet, food production is lagging behind. Secondly, the figures would look a good deal worse if they were based on an adequate diet for all.

The first thing that I would therefore like to emphasize is that this Freedom from Hunger Campaign is not just a morally laudable idea in a good cause, it is a vitally necessary international effort for the benefit of the future populations of the world.

In order to make any impression on the overall situation

the Campaign, together with the FAO, has four things to do:

1. It must survey the areas where food is inadequate and establish whether it is due to malnutrition or to under-nutrition.

2. It must settle on an acceptable remedy. By this I mean that the extra good must be acceptable to the taste and religious convictions of the people. It's no good saying that cattle will improve the protein diet in a Hindu country for instance, or that pigs should be raised by Moslems. It's almost like suggesting that the English would do better on haggis.

3. It must survey and establish the physical problems in the way of producing any acceptable remedy. Soil conditions, climate, pests, irrigation, drainage and general agricultural techniques all have a most important bearing on results.

4. It must set about the difficulty of getting its ideas adopted in the face of ignorance, prejudice, superstition and plain hostility. This is the real crux of the problem because any alteration in the cycle of primitive agriculture causes reverberations throughout an established pattern of existence which may have very serious consequences. It's no good scientists getting impatient because their ideas are not immediately accepted. Change is certainly necessary but it must be introduced with tact and understanding.

The National Agriculture Advisory Service know all about these difficulties as a result of their dealings with some farmers in this country.

I am quite sure that many people looking at this problem will be wondering why it is that we cannot simply transfer the surpluses from one area of the world to those areas where there are deficiencies. This is possible and it is being done, but it is essentially a short-term solution, both practically and economically. In the long run the proper solution must be for the people to grow the bulk of the food they need in their own areas and to pay out of their earned income for anything extra they may need.

Charity and hand-outs are for the inevitable emergencies but as permanent features in a nation's economy they become demoralizing and degrading.

This means a long-term education and training programme. It means human assistance in the form of instructors and research workers and technological assistance in the form of agricultural machinery and scientific instruments. Money by itself is not much use when people need considerate guidance and practical instruction.

The Freedom from Hunger Campaign is only intended to run for a limited time and then the United Kingdom Committee and all its organizations and experience will be disbanded, but the problems of world food production are going to be with us for generations.

I would like to suggest that the United Kingdom Committee takes steps to establish an Institute of Tropical Agriculture here in Britain. I suggest tropical agriculture because temperate agriculture already gets a great deal of attention and because virtually all the projects started by the Campaign are in tropical areas.

The functions of the Institute would be to act as a clearing house for all enquiries and information to do with tropical agriculture. To act as the link between the experimenters and the users, so that research findings could be transmitted to people who might use them, and also as a channel through which questions might be directed to the appropriate research worker. To act as the connection between the people who are working in the field and in the training centres on the one hand and the equipment makers, the seed growers, the fertilizer and machinery manufacturers on the other.

Perhaps its most important function would be to look after the interests of the field workers and experts working abroad, either under contract to tropical countries or sent out under some assistance plan. There are many British people with a great deal of experience of tropical conditions who would be only too willing to offer their services, but there is no organization to place them in the right jobs or to look after them between jobs.

The Institute would not be responsible directly for any research or teaching establishments; these already exist in considerable numbers. But it would ensure a co-ordination of effort between all agencies involved in tropical food and agricultural problems.

As an expert body on all these problems it would also be a most valuable agency for the newly formed Department of Technical co-operation. Above all it would keep alive and active the fund of goodwill and generous help stimulated by the Freedom from Hunger Campaign.

Incidentally before this suggestion is thrown out on its ear, I would earnestly recommend that the commercial advantages of such an institute should be given a little thought.

Before the Campaign can initiate any further projects or ideas it must arrange for more and more people to become aware of the world's food situation and the future prospects. This means a comprehensive effort by every person and organization concerned with these problems to get the situation across to the public at large.

As understanding spreads so must the Campaign recruit the interest and support for useful and practical projects in those parts of the world which need them most urgently.

1st May 1964.
Speech at the Welsh College of Advanced Technology.
Cardiff.

The Freedom from Hunger Campaign has caught the national imagination. There is no other way to describe the tremendous response by every kind of person and organization to this five-year campaign.

Here in Wales some 100 committees are hard at work and their success can be measured by the fact that they have extracted or accepted – whichever way you like to look at it – an average of two shillings from each one of the 2.5 million Welsh men and women and children. I gather that there are hopes that this has not quite exhausted the charitable feelings of the Welsh population and that an average of four shillings – bringing the total to £500,000 – might still be possible by the end of 1965.

I'm sure everyone here appreciates what a lot of hard and usually thankless work this is going to mean. I hope you can do it but I'm not taking any bets. I want you all to know how much your work, both of committees and individuals, is appreciated and to congratulate you on what you have achieved so far. You may be poorer in pocket, but I hope you feel richer in spirit.

The money which has been collected is not being swallowed up in some great anonymous machine operating remote and mysterious schemes. The money from Wales is going into some thirty projects which are known or should be known to every contributor.

These include such projects as the Agricultural College in Swaziland, sponsored by Cardiff and started by Lord De La Warr; a blast-freezer for fish storage in British Guyana, agricultural travel scholarships for North Borneo, animal disease investigation in Ethiopia, fishing gear for St Helena, dairies for Basutoland, agricultural engineering workshops for Southern Rhodesia and so on.

It must be fairly obvious to everyone that starvation is due to lack of food, but simple distribution of charitable food supplies is not going to solve the problem for long. The hungry must be fed, but this must be done in such a way that the present situation does not re-appear as soon as the campaign comes to an end.

The projects chosen by the United Nations Food and Agriculture Organization, in conjunction with the National Committees, are all designed to break the vicious circle which exists in so many parts of Asia and Africa. Hunger, disease, apathy, ignorance, poor farming, low yields, hunger and so on.

Compassion should be the motive for the campaign but hard-headed realism must control its execution. Every penny needs to be made to work to the best advantage, taking all the human foibles and weaknesses into consideration. It is a great mistake to imagine that the receiver feels quite the same way about charity as the provider.

For a lasting solution to world food problems we must take a hard, unblinkered look into the whole structure of human life on this earth, and attempt to recognize without prejudice where the difficulties begin.

This is not going to be easy because whereas since the beginning of time natural disasters, wars, famines and disease have kept the human population in check, now mankind has got virtually all these restraints under control. We now have a much tighter grip upon our environment and therefore the responsibility for our destiny is almost entirely in our own hands. We can't go on tinkering with odd bits of our existence and then ignore its consequences. It really is about time we took our responsibilities much more seriously and recognized their full scope.

This campaign is a step in the right direction. At least we've learned that, however worthy charity may be as a principle, it must be tempered with common sense in practice. This campaign is a genuine attempt to make sure that in our well-meaning attempts to help we do not create an even more difficult situation. Even so, a realistic glimpse of the future is rather gloomy.

By the year 2000 it is predicted that the world population will have doubled from what it is now and reached a total of some 6,000 million people. In order to feed the extra mouths, agricultural production will have to go up by some 200 per cent and that will only maintain the present standards of nutrition. Even to maintain the present hopelessly inadequate standards of education, housing and medical care will require tremendous exertion on the part of all mankind. If this enormous increase is going to take place we must obviously do everything we can to cope with its problems but I think it is important that we should not delude ourselves about what is going on.

This campaign is the first co-ordinated attempt to tackle world problems on a world scale. Let's hope its success leads to more ambitious plans and ultimately to a much pleasanter world for its inhabitants, wherever they may live.

Extract from 'Men, Machines and Sacred Cows', published in 1984 by Hamish Hamilton, London.

The point about food aid is that it is intended to make up the deficiency in food production in the receiving country and is not simply a free gift to the consumer. Consequently, if it is not to put the small producer out of business, the proper recipient of the gift of food should be the food producer who can then sell it, together with his own produce, so that he is provided with an increased income and the consumer with an increased supply of food.

It may well be that the troubles of the EEC's Common Agricultural Policy have their origins in the failure to identify these problems correctly in the first place. Just because food is common to producers and consumers does not mean that it poses the same problems to both. Yet the interests of both are supposed to be the responsibility of the same authority. Furthermore, by subsidizing the prices paid to all producers and the prices paid by all consumers, rather than the needy individuals, a whole new series of problems has been created.

If, as seems likely, one of the intentions of the CAP is to benefit the small and relatively disadvantaged producer by putting a price on his product that will keep him in business, the inevitable consequence is that the bigger, and probably more efficient producer will cash in on this bonanza; the result is massive over-production at a very great cost to the taxpayer. Incidentally, it also creates an awkward problem for the authority in disposing of these unwanted stocks.

19th May 1985.
Address to the Council Meeting of the World Wildlife Fund.
Divonne, France.

As far as my own other activities during the last year are concerned, by far the most interesting was a visit to six countries in Africa. It was one of the most depressing journeys I have ever experienced. These countries are not wealthy and both the climate and the geography are harsh, making it difficult for all forms of life to survive at the best of times. The situation would have been bad enough, but it has been made very much worse by fourteen years of more or less severe drought. The tragedy and the irony is that in many ways the situation is a result of an intensive programme of aid and development. The fact is that the programme has been spectacularly successful in terms of human population growth. Both the human population and the populations of domestic livestock have doubled in the last twenty-five years. If present trends are allowed to continue (of course, one does not know what effect the drought is going to have) they will double again in the next twenty-three years. The sad fact is that, instead of the same number of people being very much better off, more than twice as many people are just as badly off as they were before. Unfortunately all this well-intentioned development has resulted in an ecological disaster of immense proportions.

Attention was first drawn to the Ethiopian famine in late 1984. Donations to provide relief were made on a huge scale. But the ecological, political, social and administrative problems, which exacerbated the effect of years of drought, could only be relieved through aid from the developed countries and a resolution of the civil wars being fought in western Ethiopia.

The Population Factor

20th May 1985.
Reply to Mr Anders Wijkman at the Council Meeting of the World
Wildlife Fund.
Divonne, France.

I would also like to thank Mr Wijkman for his very interesting address. He has thrown a new and welcome light on the whole issue of human existence in Africa. I sympathize with most of his valuable contributions but I would like to make a few comments on some of the points he raised.

I think that Mr Wijkman's point that natural events only become disasters when they are the cause of death and destruction to mankind, is very important. After all, you cannot really blame the sea when sailors are stupid enough to become shipwrecked. His other point that mankind can, and does, create ecological disasters is equally important.

I am very glad that he drew attention to the fact that in Africa, wood accounts for 60 per cent of the total energy consumption. The majority of that, of course, is for cooking. This is the cause of a serious dilemma, since any increase in the supply of food, whether imported, donated or home grown, means an increased demand for fuel wood.

Mr Wijkman mentioned that 'only Africa has had a fall in the production of food' but I think it needs to be emphasized that he said 'per capita'. Total food production has in fact risen, but not as fast as the growth of the human population. Therefore, to be realistic, we ought to look at it the other way round. The food is there but there are far too many people trying to consume it.

He also suggested that many problems have been caused by well-intentioned development and aid projects. It is often said that many economic problems have been created by the collapse of commodity prices. The irony is that many of these commodities have been produced as a result of aid programmes and it is one of the facts of economic life that when supply goes up, prices are likely to come down.

Incidentally, I can't help wondering whether we are really justified in our attempts to solve African problems. I just wonder how we would react, for instance, to African intervention in some of our social problems, such as drugs, crime, hooliganism and unemployment? Perhaps we ought to take the beam out of our own eye before we bother about the speck in our brother's eye.

I think that his questions about disaster relief are very much to the point. It is the soup–kitchen problem on a grand scale. Once you have established a free source of supply, how do you persuade people to start fending for themselves again? And what happens when their ability to fend for themselves is somehow or other destroyed?

He referred to the major inter-linked factors behind the disasters. I can't help saying that I see them in a rather different order of priority. In my opinion, short–sighted aid and development programmes have led to a much too rapid rate of population growth, which in turn has led to the breakdown of the traditional social and agricultural fabric and ultimately to ecological degradation. I am not convinced that 'environmental degradation is caused by poor land use and short–sighted exploitation of natural resources' alone. If that were to be so, why is it that it has only occurred now after thousands of years of human occupation?

I am all for 'disaster prevention', as I think we all are, but I would dearly like to know how this is to be achieved.

Incidentally, I would question whether the rural popu-lations are more vulnerable to disasters than the inhabitants of cities. People displaced from rural areas as a result of drought, or over-population, find their way to the cities and end up in slum conditions, with all the attendant risks of disease, unemployment and social breakdown. Their only immediate advantage is that good aid is more likely to be available, provided of course that the distribution system actually works. If the supply of food from outside should fail, the result would be catastrophic.

I sympathize with Prince Sadruddin's comments on roads. I once made a very similar point to the Prime Minister of Malaysia, Tunku Abdul Rahman. His reply was, 'If you put a road into a village, the merchants go up it and the villagers come down it and go to the nearest city.' And that is where the nearest aid is.

However, thanks to the very generous food aid, the drought has not yet created a general famine in the western part of central Africa, but the fact has to be faced that, even if there is enough food, double the population consumes double the fuel wood and double the livestock population consumes double the natural pasture. So, quite apart from this severe over-exploitation of the fragile natural resources, it is exactly the trees and the pasture that are suffering most seriously from the drought. On top of all this, wildlife is being poached at a destructive rate. It is really difficult to avoid the conclusion that an irreversible run-down situation has now been reached.

A combination of all these factors has had the effect of allowing the desert to encroach further and further into what had been marginal land. In parts of Mauritania the desert is said to be advancing at the rate of six kilometres a year. I saw for myself the advancing sand dunes to the west of the Air Mountains in northern Niger. Some of the trees have been so recently engulfed that their upper branches are still showing above the sand. Some of them, very hardy acacias, were still putting out green shoots even though they were almost drowned by sand.

I may say that the trees which have so far not been drowned, are not much better off. The nomadic stockmen have always used the technique for cutting branches from trees so that their flocks can get at the green shoots. Under normal circumstances the trees can survive this treatment, but the absence of any other pasture, as a result of the drought, has meant that the rate of cutting has greatly increased and, as the trees themselves are suffering from the drought, the majority will not survive for very much longer. And, needless to say, no young trees are growing at all.

Drought inevitably implies lack of water and the obvious answer is of course to dig wells, or to make existing wells deeper. It sounds splendid, but unfortunately it ignores the fact that if you extract more water from underground, the water table is inclined to be lowered with the result that the roots of the trees cannot reach it any more.

It seems to me that many of the well-intentioned development programmes have suffered from this lack of foresight, or lack of consideration of the practical consequences. The trouble appears to be that the plans are drawn up against the ecological background of a temperate climate and the social structures of the people who live in them. West and Central Africa are very different in both respects. The ecology is very fragile and the social structures and habits of the inhabitants are the outcome of many thousands of years of trying to survive under these very harsh and adverse conditions. I suspect that disregard for these facts has been the reason for the failure of so many grand development projects. I think this is particularly true of the great irrigation schemes which have demanded that people who have been tribal and nomadic stock-rearers for thousands of years should suddenly become collectivized, industrial farm workers. Evidence seems to suggest, as we have heard already, that small-scale irrigation schemes are more likely to be successful than the very big and ambitious projects.

Even with a return to what might be normal rainfall, it is difficult to see how these natural resources of pasture, tree cover and wildlife can ever fully recover. Many of the natural plant and pasture species may well be extinct by then and even with massive afforestation programmes, it is a fact of life that trees take some forty years to become useful. Furthermore, attempts to take short cuts, by planting what are said to be quick-maturing exotic trees, will merely cause even more ecological problems, since they are virtually useless to the natural fauna, and are not necessarily adapted to the local ecological pattern of seasonal variation.

One of the most discouraging aspects is the dreadful imbalance between funds for development and funds for any form of conservation. I attended a discussion in Nouakchott, the capital of Mauritania. (Incidentally, the city was built as the capital when the country became independent in 1960 and it was planned for a population of 30,000. The population has already been swollen to 300,000 by refugees from the drought. They of course are living in slums and you can imagine what is happening to whatever supply of wood there was in the vicinity of that town.) In the course of the discussion in Nouakchott, I asked the representative from the European Development Fund how much he was planning to spend on development projects this year. The answer was in the region of $10 million. I then asked the Directeur de la Protection de la Nature what his budget was. The answer was a paltry $20,000. I would like to say that one of the best essays on the conservation situation in West Africa was given to us by the Directeur of that department. One wonders why it is that all his development money has got to go into projects that *we* invent instead of supporting the activities which are obviously generated at home.

I notice that one of the chapters in *Famine* – the book Prince Sadruddin is promoting – is called 'Ad-Hocracy'. It seems to me a very good word and it could be applied to a great number of the activities in the development world. I am quite convinced that, as Mr Wijkman said, there is an urgent need for all agencies, whether Governmental or voluntary, to co-operate and to co-ordinate their activities in the long-term interests of the people of Africa. My only reservation is that we should all stick to the things we know about and can do best. There is certainly a human tragedy unfolding in certain parts of Africa, but it will not be made any better if we all rush in trying to solve what appear to be the most obvious and immediate human problems. We must not forget that there is also an ecological tragedy unfolding and that is our business. This raises the question of what we should be doing about it. I believe that we in WWF and our partners in IUCN should be following five broad avenues of activity:

We should support and encourage those governments which are sympathetic to our objectives, who understand the purposes of conservation, and who understand and sympathize with what we are trying to do. They need constant confirmation that they are doing the right thing. All the development agencies are going to try to persuade them to do something else, or to ignore the needs of conservation because it gets in the way of their development projects, so that they really need to have it confirmed to them that they *are* doing the right thing, no matter how difficult it may be for them to sustain their resolve. And that requires frequent visits to stiffen their resolve and their morale.

Secondly, I think we must seek to convince other governments which are not sympathetic and don't understand the problems that conservation of nature is essential to the future welfare of their people. Of course this requires more frequent visits, not to confirm them in their resolution but to change their resolution and to support conservation.

Thirdly, I think we must seek in some way to influence government and non-government aid agencies and lenders of money, at least to consult the Conservation for Development Centre about the ecological consequences of their plans before putting them into effect.[3] The number of occasions when plans have been shown to be disastrous after they have been embarked on, after the planning has taken place, when the planners have either then gone ahead or had to send the plans back to be reworked, is legion. It would be so much easier if people would only take the ecological consequences into consideration and ask for advice beforehand from the people who know what they are talking about. How do you do this? Obviously through personal contact with the people who are in this world of aid agencies and banks, and by somehow infiltrating their conferences and discussions.

I think the fourth corollary to all this is that we should give moral support and encouragement to family planning organizations and projects. It may cause us to feel uncomfortable – it may be a social problem, a religious problem or a political problem, but it is a fact of life. You simply cannot avoid the fact that, without some long-term way of restricting the rate of increase in the population, there cannot be any long-term improvement. For every development programme in the absence of control over the population increase, will merely succeed in maintaining more people at a poverty level. There will be no net gain in standards, and you will only get a net loss to the natural environment.

Lastly, and above all, we must remember our primary objective, and ensure that our conservation projects in the area, which we undertake jointly with IUCN, are properly planned, properly co-ordinated, properly financed and staffed and then properly supported.

I believe that WWF and IUCN must continue to concern themselves with the conservation of nature and wildlife. For one thing, if we don't do it, no one else will, and some organization must ensure that at least a reservoir of wild plants and animals survives to take their rightful place in the long-term life of the continent, against the day when the other agencies have managed, we hope, to relieve the human problems.

Culling and Control of
Wild Populations

18th February 1981.
Address to the All-Party Conservation Committee.
London.

Strange as it may seem, conservation itself causes conservation problems. Protection of a species or a habitat may easily – and frequently does – create a problem of over-population which consequently upsets the balance of nature. Although isolated groups of animals are better than none, there are dangers in the inevitable reduction in the size of the gene pool of that particular species. The management of such situations is fraught with difficulties. It is not easy to persuade people who have subscribed money to save such and such an animal that some of them need to be killed. Proposals to cull the greatly increased numbers of seals on the east coast have met with furious opposition. There is a major row going on in South America at the moment about the killing of vicuna in a national park. There are arguments about the number of the animals in the park, which lead to arguments about the numbers to be culled, who should cull, how they should be culled and who should pay for the whole thing.

Then there is the problem of disease. Wild populations are frequently reservoirs for diseases that affect man and domestic animals. Measures designed to control sleepy sickness in Africa have had a devastating effect on wildlife.

In this country, evidence has been produced that cattle and badgers in some areas of certain counties in the South-West suffer from tuberculosis and that they re-infect each other. While it seems quite acceptable for cattle found to be suffering from tuberculosis to be slaughtered, there is understandably a great outcry about any attempt to use a similar method to eradicate – or at least to control the spread of – the disease among the wild badger population in that area. The unfortunate part about it is that no one has yet found an alternative to gassing badger setts suspected of harbouring infected animals.[4] Neither is it possible to establish for certain whether a badger family is suffering from the disease before deciding to kill it. The decision has to be made on circumstantial evidence.

23rd November 1973.
The 4th Jane Hodge Memorial Lecture, The Institute of Science and Technology.
Cardiff.

'Conservation against nature' may sound like a contradiction but the problem arises simply because it is no longer possible to ensure large enough undisturbed areas in which the natural balances of nature can operate satisfactorily in keeping the various wild populations under control.

A very typical example is the Tsavo National Park in East Africa, where natural and human predation of the elephant stock was suddenly stopped when it was made a National Park, with the result that the elephants suffered a population explosion and were well on their way to changing the whole ecology of the park. It was therefore proposed that the population should be controlled by cropping, but this was not universally acceptable for a number of reasons. In the end the problem was solved by a very severe drought which drastically reduced the number of elephants in the park.

Altogether the control of pests, whether by shooting, trapping, poisoning or artificially induced disease or sterility and predation, is a very difficult issue. In most cases pests are simply wild populations which we do not like for one reason or another, and it is a strange quirk of human morality that while some object to the killing of some animals and many abhor the use of so-called inhumane methods of killing others, no one seems to mind how pests are controlled. Furthermore, there is an entirely irrational concern based on the size or the appeal of the animal. The rule is that the smaller or the uglier the animal the less concern there is about its fate.

Inevitably, the conservationist is most concerned with those species which are in danger of extinction and with their habitats, but what no one knows for certain is whether the species would, left to itself, be dying out from natural causes or whether it is due to human interference.

Perhaps the most difficult problem is to decide to what extent conservation measures are themselves interfering with the process of evolution and natural selection. A wild population will have evolved to its present state as a result of the conditions and pressures under which it has tried to exist. If those pressures are suddenly removed or changed, the selection of those strains which are most suitable for the conditions is also changed and it is quite possible to lose important characteristics within relatively few generations.

18th February 1981.
Address to the All-Party Conservation Committee.
London.

Furthermore, good conservation practice may entail what is termed 'culling' and this can cause serious conflict between people otherwise devoted to the principles of conservation. At the moment there is the case of the vicunas in Peru. The scientists working at Pampa Galeras claim that there are 44,000 of them and that they need to be culled. However, an aerial survey commissioned by those who think that they should not be culled puts the figure between 15 and 18,000. In my experience anyone who tries to restore peace between arguing conservationists usually comes off worst of all.

Much the same applies to foresters in the developed countries. Of course some animals are nuisances and any species can become a pest if its population gets too big, but there is a great difference between trying to exterminate a pest and learning to live with a nuisance.

Much as some people would like, it is really not possible to prevent every instance of human interference with the natural environment or every case of the exploitation of wild populations. It may well be distasteful to kill baby seals, but provided the species as a whole, or any branch of it, is not threatened with extinction itself, or is threatening the extinction of another species, it is not a conservation problem. It may be a moral problem, but it cannot, for example, rate a higher priority than the protection of a species from extinction, even if the threat to the survival of a species is posed by morally less offensive activities, such as drainage schemes, commercial fishing or the cropping of forest areas.

4th June 1982.
The Chancellor's Lecture, Salford University.

Anxiety to help can also get a bit confused. For instance there is a big difference between the methods used to exploit wild resource species on the one hand and the threat to the extinction of species on the other. There are those who are primarily concerned with animal welfare and they object to the methods used to kill whales; and there are the conservationists who object to the killing of such a great number of whales because it threatens some species with extinction. In this case of course the interests of animal welfare and conservation coincide. In the case of the Canadian seal cull, the animal welfare groups object to the methods used to cull the seals, while the conservationists are primarily concerned to see that the permitted level of cull does not threaten any of the seal species with the risk of extinction, or that the knock-on effect of either protection or exploitation does not affect other species in the system. The problem is to establish acceptable figures; naturally conservationists always look on the pessimistic side, and I think there is very serious concern about some of the Canadian seal populations.

Animal welfare groups get annoyed by conservationists who appear to be reluctant to support some of their campaigns. The reason is simply that in view of the huge list of species in danger of extinction, the priority task of a conservation organization must be to concern itself with these threatened species and with their habitats. On the other hand conservationists sometimes get impatient with animal welfare groups for diverting public attention from threatened but perhaps less glamorous or appealing animals to others in no danger of extinction. In any case it is not possible to provide protection for a truly wild species unless its whole habitat is protected and of course habitat protection raises a rather different series of problems to that of the welfare of any particular species.

Extract from an Article in 'The Shooting Life', London, 1987.

The object of the WWF is to 'conserve' the system as a whole; not to prevent the killing of individual animals. Those who are concerned about the conservation of nature accept that all species are prey to some other species. They accept that most species produce a surplus that is capable of being culled without in any way threatening the survival of the species as a whole.

The absolutely vital point is that no more than the surplus should be taken, so that there is always a sufficient breeding population left to produce the surplus for the following year. This applies to game species in exactly the same way as it does to sea fisheries or to domestic flocks and herds. The reason why domestic animal and plant species are not in danger of becoming extinct is that they are somebody's property, and it is in the owner's interest to protect them from being rustled or poached.

Many people have an objection to the rearing of game birds later to be shot for sport. This is an ethical argument and it has no conservation significance. Neither is it against what might be described as the world's 'natural system' which, among other things, provides for the maintenance of a balance between predators and prey; between the production of edible forage and the demand by the consumers. Danger only occurs when the predator becomes too successful and drives its prey to the verge of extinction. Under natural conditions the prey is very unlikely to become completely extinct since that would put the predator's own survival at risk.

The conclusion of all this is that the 'cropping' of a wild population in such a way that a sufficient breeding population is always left to produce a surplus for the following year, causes no harm or danger to the survival of the prey species. However it does mean that all such cropping or culling activities have to be properly controlled to ensure that a viable breeding population is kept intact. These controls need to be applied by national legislation, but, while they will be observed by the law-abiding section of the population, poachers, by definition, do not abide by the law. Therefore the effectiveness of the legislation depends on the vigour and efficiency of the law enforcement agency. It is unfortunate, but there are many countries where both the law and its enforcement are wholly inadequate to provide the necessary protection to commercially valuable species and the control over protected areas.

One of the most important ways of achieving the conservation of endangered species is to set aside, or to create, suitable habitat areas. Such areas then become habitats for any number of other wild species. When the population of tigers in India was threatened with extinction some 15 years ago, WWF persuaded the Indian Government to embark on a conservation programme. This consisted of declaring a number of National Parks where tigers could be protected from hunters and poachers. Ironically, most of these Parks happened to be areas which had previously been game reserves set aside by the Maharajahs.

Much the same occurs in many European countries where there is game shooting. Areas set aside as game coverts and wetlands maintained for wildfowl are also refuges for a great many wild species, both native and migratory. The difference in the look of the countryside between those areas where game shooting takes place and those areas which are used exclusively for agriculture is immediately apparent. In the latter case there are no small woods, no hedgerows, no wet areas and no little rough places, and it is most noticeable that little or no birdlife is evident at all.

Trouble can also occur when two predators are competing for the same prey. Take the grouse, for instance. It is a bird species that occurs entirely in the wild and only in the British Isles. It depends on heather for its survival and it is virtually impossible to breed sufficient numbers in captivity to stock the moors. Its main predator is man – the grouse shooter – but it also happens to be a very tasty morsel for foxes, crows, falcons and eagles. The obvious solution has been to employ gamekeepers to limit the number of the natural predators. There is no harm in that, except that gamekeepers can become too efficient. In Scotland, the gamekeepers and the sheep farmers between them nearly accomplished the extinction of the golden eagle. Paradoxically, it is not the shooter's prey which is at risk, but the natural predators of the shooter's prey which come under the greatest pressure.

People may have differing views about the killing of animals for sport, but provided it is done with care and consideration for the survival of the prey species and for the survival of its natural predators, it poses no particular threat. Indeed, as it is obviously in the interest of law-abiding shooters to ensure that they have a prey for the next season, they become natural conservationists. The only danger is that in their enthusiasm to give their prey species the very best chance to breed a sizeable surplus each year, they may inadvertently put the survival of other predator, or vermin, species at risk of extinction. The trouble with the poacher is that he is in it for a quick commercial return, and not at all interested in the long-term conservation of his prey.

Captive Breeding in Zoos

24th April 1972.
Speech to Open the New Lecture Hall at Chester Zoological Gardens.

I think that anybody who is interested in animals is bound to be interested in zoos, and I think anybody who is interested in zoos in this country has heard of Chester Zoo.

It so happens that I have been President of the London Zoological Society for a number of years and so I have even better reason to know and to admire the standards, at second-hand, so to speak, of this zoo.

I was interested to hear about the very delicate balance that has to be kept between the interests of the animals and the interests of the visitors. A lot of visitors to zoos are convinced that the cages are put up to keep the animals in. Everybody in the zoo world knows perfectly well they are merely to keep the visitors out.

This is not an easy time for wild animals, and it is not an easy time for zoos. Animals have always been the cause of pretty deep emotions in this country, and now that the whole business of the conservation of nature has become such a popular issue, the path between emotionalism and commercialism is rather narrow and very tricky. Reputable zoological gardens were performing a useful function long before people became interested in conservation. I don't think they have ever tried to exploit the display of animals for commercial profit and most of them have been deeply concerned from the very first with the welfare and scientific study of their collections.

Indeed, it was only some years ago that most of the reputable zoos in most parts of the world agreed together that they would not deal in any animals on the endangered list, except, of course, those individuals which were bred within the zoological gardens themselves.

Then, more recently, the zoos in this country, because of the growing number of zoological gardens and places where animals are put on display, formed a federation of zoos in an attempt to inspect and control the standards of these places. Unfortunately it was not quite as successful as it should have been, but as a result of the activities of the federation, there is now legislation in the pipeline to create a zoological council which will have the powers to control the standards of establishments, in fact to do the things which the federation set out to do and with which the federation will be very closely associated.

The main thing is that all our zoos have shown that they do make a very important contribution to conservation. For instance by breeding rare animals in captivity and keeping them, so to speak, safe until a reasonably safe or reasonable wild home can be found for them. This has happened on a number of occasions where animals have been bred in zoos and then eventually put back into their original homes where the wild stock had completely died out.

Then by studying breeding habits, food requirements, diseases and behavioural characteristics. This research will also make it possible, not only to keep animals in zoos, but to help those animals to continue to exist in the wild, in areas where the situation is becoming rather difficult for them, where the area has been reduced and where there are all sorts of other factors which make it difficult for them to survive. The things that the zoos learn will be very helpful in keeping the wild population going.

Most important of all, by their educational programmes, by their efforts to educate both young and old in this whole broad field of natural history.

Lots of people can get excited about the conservation of nature and by the problems of the natural environment, but it is only those who understand the principles and the problems of conservation and the existence and the life of wild animals who can do very much about it, who can make any reasonable contribution.

23rd May 1973.
Address at the Annual General Meeting of the Zoological Society of London.

Over the past several years the change in general attitudes to animals, wildlife and the natural and human environment has been quite dramatic. In the first place, most of the specialist bodies concerned with the study of conservation of particular species, or groups of animals or plants, or geographical areas, all started to notice independently that things were beginning to go wrong at about the same time – roughly during the 1950s. The outcome was the foundation of the World Wildlife Fund followed by the first 'Countryside in 1970' conference, which fully confirmed suspicions that the countryside in this country and wildlife all over the world were facing serious trouble.

It is becoming quite apparent that a very large number of animals and plants simply cannot coexist with human occupation of land. They are not compatible with intensive cultivation, dense urbanization or industrialization. In some cases overlapping is possible, particularly in water and in the air. The problem of conservation is therefore that the direct protection of individual species is not really effective except under zoo conditions. If wildlife is to continue, whole areas will need to be set aside and the wild population contained and managed within them in such a way that people can see the animals without disturbing their natural existence more than is absolutely necessary. The great African parks show that this can be done very effectively.

If this is an acceptable theory, it raises the rather interesting idea that zoological gardens and collections are beginning to come closer to conservation areas. Both depend on the principle of the direct management of wildlife. The only major difference is that zoos collect from all over the world, whereas conservation areas are concerned with the protection of indigenous species.

There are, of course, certain special considerations which will have to be taken into account in the management of wildlife protected areas. Migration is an obvious example, and wild populations which are used as a source of food or for commercial or sporting purposes will also need very particular treatment.

The notion that all wildlife will have to be specially managed in order to allow it to survive at all, raises some other rather interesting ideas.

Human mobility has become such that it might be asked whether, in the long run, it would not be better for all concerned if people were to go where the animals are at home rather than trying to bring the animals to where the people are at home. In any case, as the pressure on wild species continues to increase, the need for special collections will be greater than it is today. In addition, the whole business of scientific study through comparative physiology and comparative medicine will become more important, while the skills and techniques of animal management in zoos will become increasingly valuable to the management of conservation areas.

8th May 1974.
Welcome to the Members of a Symposium Organized by 'The 1001:
A Nature Trust'.
London Zoo.

Every symposium, conference or convention has to have an opening session and an opening speaker. Speaking from personal experience, the less one knows about the subject the better. I think I could nearly claim to be a professional opening speaker (I say 'nearly' because I do not get paid for it – perhaps 'career opening speaker' might be a better description), but on this occasion it so happens that I have four very good reasons for speaking first and for offering you all a very hearty welcome to London Zoo.

In the first place, I am President of the Zoological Society of London, and for that you can blame the Honorary Secretary, Lord Zuckerman. Second, I am President of the British National Appeal of the World Wildlife Fund – for that you can blame Sir Peter Scott, who is responsible for all the arrangements for this meeting. Third, I am an International Trustee of the World Wildlife Fund, for which you can blame my colleague, Prince Bernhard, whom we are all very happy to have with us today.

Fourth and finally, I am a member of the 1001 Trust for which you can thank the moral persuasion of the President of the World Wildlife Fund. This Trust owes its success very much to his initiative and enthusiasm, ably assisted by Charles de Haes – they have done a marvellous job catching so many big fish.

It is absolutely essential to see that the younger generations learn about their natural environment as a normal part of their education, but first they must have the facts. Only then can we expect them to give their hearts and minds to conservation. Industrialism has become such a powerful influence on contemporary life, and particularly on modern education, that many important aspects of existence on this planet are being ignored. Science, technology and vocational training courses have displaced the study of our natural environment and man's relationship to it. As a result, for the very great majority of those who live in the big cities, the first contact with the wild animals of the world is made in zoos. Wild animals in captivity are not simply an entertainment or a sort of side-show; they form an essential link between urban man, completely cut off from nature in the ordinary sense, and all his fellow living creatures, who are finding it increasingly difficult to share this planet with him.

The protection of wild species, and especially those which are in danger of extinction, can be accomplished in two ways: in the wild and in captivity.

I suspect that most members of the 1001 Trust have a pretty good understanding of the problems of protecting endangered species in the wild. The programme arranged for you today is intended to explain what zoological societies are doing to help the survival of rare species. The problems are different, and the approach is different, but it can be very effective and it should be seen as complementary to the main effort of the World Wildlife Fund.

The Population Factor

1st July 1983.
*Address on Receiving Honorary Degree from the University of
Western Ontario. Canada.*

Zoological gardens throughout the world are now collaborating in the breeding of endangered species in captivity. In some cases so as to obviate the temptation for them to capture wild specimens, and in other cases so as to re-establish the species in the wild. The Arabian oryx, which had become extinct in Arabia, has now been reintroduced in Oman and the indications are that the project is a success.

Zoos are not without their critics, but the idea of farming what are considered to be wild animals for the sake of their products raises the emotional temperature much higher. However, from a strictly conservation point of view it is obviously preferable to farm animals, if that is likely to save them from extinction in the wild as a result of poaching or even legal killing or capture.

IV

THE VICTIMS

The ever increasing human population and the inevitable growth in its demand for natural resources, coupled with the environmental consequences of human activities, has had, and is continuing to have, a very significant effect on the world's natural system. There are individual casualties when a species becomes extinct, but the cumulative effect is much more serious.

I suppose it might be theoretically possible for the human species to survive with nothing but domestic plants and animals, but it is doubtful whether such a situation could go on for very long. For instance, it would only take a disease such as myxomatosis to strike domestic cattle for serious problems to confront the human population.

One of the key factors in the health of the natural system is genetic diversity. Nature's answer to natural disasters is the variation in the genetic 'make-up' between species within a genus and between subspecies or races within species. Whenever something has gone seriously wrong, there has always been a sufficient choice of alternatives capable of adapting to the new situation. Some subspecies may have a greater resistance to a certain disease, which gives them a better chance of survival, should the disease strike the main population.

The world has experienced various kinds of natural disasters often enough, but it has never had to cope with the continuing erosion of the health and vitality of the whole of its web of life. The really baleful influence of the sheer size of the human species is in creating a severe imbalance in the natural system. It is reducing genetic diversity by causing the extinction of species; it is interfering with the balance of nature and it is also interfering with the even more delicate climatic balance. Most animal life depends on the availability of oxygen in the atmosphere. Oxygen is produced by plants absorbing carbon dioxide from the atmosphere and, with the help of energy from the sun, converting it into carbohydrates for their own use and releasing oxygen into the atmosphere for the use of animals. Human activities, such as industry and power generation, produce large quantities of carbon dioxide. The seas absorb much of this gas, but the major converters are the great tropical forests. These are being destroyed at an alarming rate, and exactly what will happen when the production of carbon dioxide exceeds the world's natural ability to convert it into oxygen and carbon is not altogether certain.

The pollution of the seas as a result of the dumping of effluents and waste products, the enclosure and drainage of coastal and tidal mudflats and marshes, and the use of damaging and wasteful fishing methods are creating similar problems for the natural economy of the oceans.

Human interference with the chemistry and the temperature of the atmosphere is also changing the structure of the climate. It is quite possible that the exceptionally long and severe droughts in so many parts of the world are due to some other cause, but the likelihood is that they are due to changes in the climate brought about by the disappearance of forests and the spread of deserts.

The immediate victims of human interference in the working of the natural system may be the wild species of animals and plants, but the ultimate victim will be the

human species itself. Unfortunately, it is in the nature of
governments only to concern themselves with the short-
term problems; but in terms of the long-term survival of
all life on earth, that is not good enough. The inexorable
laws of nature dictate that any species can only expand to
the point at which its numbers threaten the health and
productivity of its own habitat. The more it destroys its
habitat, the more certain it is that it will destroy itself.

Animals

11th May 1982.
Speech to the Council for Environmental Conservation Conference.
London.

It is easy to assume that conservation is a relatively new phenomenon. After all, the International Union for the Conservation of Nature and Natural Resources was only founded in 1948, and even the oldest of the Natural History societies have not been going for much over 100 years. The World Wildlife Fund was only founded less than 25 years ago, yet you may recall that Noah started it all umpteen thousand years ago with his ark. Even then he was presumably too late to save the dinosaurs, unless there were several arks.

The difference with Noah is that he was saving the animals from a disaster deliberately organized by the Almighty against the unruly and sinful human population. Conservationists today are trying to save them from a human-created disaster, not from just a single flood but from two revolutions and an explosion. The Industrial Revolution, the scientific revolution and the human population explosion.

The effect of all this on the world's wildlife has been nothing short of catastrophic. The stories of the extermination of the dodo and the passenger pigeon, and the near extermination of the plains bison are only too well known, but the consequences of that sort of wanton destruction were recognized at the time. It proved too late to save the passenger pigeon, but in the case of the plains bison steps were taken to save it from extinction, but only just in time.

As a matter of interest, as early as 1874 a bill was passed by both houses of Congress to 'impose a penalty on every man, red, white or black, who might wantonly kill buffaloes'. I am sorry to say that it was vetoed by President Grant.

9th March 1983.
Speech to the Vancouver Canadian Club.

It is the extinction of species that is the first and over-riding priority of conservation. Concern for the welfare of animals in general and anxiety about the methods used to kill both wild and domestic animals in particular, are most desirable and admirable, but when it comes to the matter of the survival of a species, the particular method responsible for making it extinct is irrelevant. Extinction, after all, is forever. The fact of the matter is that a remnant population will be made extinct whether the last surviving individuals are clubbed, shot, trapped, poisoned or find their habitat taken over for agriculture, industry or housing. Where a population is big enough and sufficiently fertile to allow a surplus to be cropped without endangering the survival of the species, the methods used to take the crop are a matter for animal welfare, not for the conservation of nature.

I firmly believe that most thinking people regret the terrible destruction of wildlife, but unless they make some positive contribution that regret is worthless.

Some people are completely unmoved; they don't want

to know about the problems of nature. They are comfort-able in their way of life and can see no practical value in the conservation of wildlife. To them I would say that the world's wildlife is like the miner's canary: if the canary died, the miner knew it was his turn next.

Let me just quote from the foreword by York Edwards to the book, *Wild Mammals of Canada*, written by Frederick Wooding:

> '*Many large mammals, and some small ones too, are unable to cope with changing North America. They vanish from watershed after watershed, country after country, mountain after mountain, with no alarm raised as long as someone knows some place where they are still to be found. When we ring the alarm it is close to the last mountain, the last valley, the last country to have them, and it is much too late.*'

If we let this process continue, future generations will have every right to ask why it was that we who are alive today allowed the natural world to become so impover-ished. What answer have we got? We can no longer claim that we are unaware of the situation. So, are we too busy worrying about other things? Are we too greedy to consider sharing this planet with our fellow creatures? Or is it that we believe that the whole thing is simply too unimportant to bother about? Is that the judgement you would like posterity to make of this generation?

7th June 1962.
Address to the World Wildlife Fund.
New York.

The Fund which is being launched tonight may well be responsible for changing the course of world history.

The World Wildlife Fund has been formed in order to try and conserve the world's rapidly diminishing wildlife of all kinds. If it succeeds our descendants will have the pleasure of seeing wild animals. If it fails they will be forced to live in a world where the only living creatures will be man himself and his domestic animals. Always assuming, of course, that we don't destroy ourselves as well in the meantime. In case any of you here are in any doubt about the need for this work, I am going to inflict some pretty convincing statistics on you.

Since the time of our Lord, and that, you will recall, is 1,962 years, about 100 animals and the same number of birds have become extinct. Species that took at least two and a half million years to develop – wiped out forever. Just in case you're still feeling a bit smug let me remind you that the passenger pigeon, which used to darken the skies of North America, was exterminated – not as a pest but just for fun – in one human generation within the last 100 years. Today there are 250 species of animals and birds in danger of extermination by the sheer callousness of mankind. Ironically, the national symbol of the world's greatest nation, the bald eagle, proud emblem of the mighty United States of America, is itself on the list. 'Father, what's that funny bird on the dollar – have you ever seen one?' 'No, my boy – we killed them off in a fit of absentmindedness.'

I am not going to bore you with the names of all 250, but it may interest you to know just why some of them are under sentence of death. The golden eagle of North

America is being chased and killed by people in light airplanes who seem to think that it is smart to have their feathers and claws. The Arabian oryx owes its fate to the fact that some Arabs believe they must prove their manhood by killing an oryx so that they will inherit its legendary courage and virility. This may have made a little sense years ago in the days when mankind was tyrannized by superstition and the odds were a bit more even; but today, when up to 300 car-borne parties go out together to get-brave-quick by mowing down oryxes with tommy-guns, the whole thing becomes sheer idiocy.

There are in fact five reasons why wild animals are in danger all over the world.

First, physical conditions are changing; human population is increasing, forcing the animals out. Industry and science are polluting the air, the soil and the water, unintentionally maybe, but none the less effectively killing off vast numbers of animals and fish.

Second, the means of controlling those creatures which are considered to be pests and nuisances are very much more powerful than ever before in history. They are in fact no longer means of control: they are methods of extermination. Even then, things might not be so bad if they only affected the so-called pests; the trouble is that they set up a chain reaction in nature which takes in many innocent creatures and in some cases man himself.

Third, there are the killers for profit, the poachers, the get-rich-quick-at-any-cost-mob. In Africa they are rapidly getting rid of the rhino because illegal dealers want the horn for China where for some incomprehensible reason they seem to think that it acts as an aphrodisiac – in China, of all places, where I should have thought that the population statistics alone would have convinced anyone that those things were quite obviously unnecessary.

Also in Africa and elsewhere, these thoughtless exploiters are slaughtering vast numbers of elephants merely because they can get fifty cents a pound for their ivory from a middle-man who sells it to a receiver for double that. He in turn gets two dollars a pound from an illegal dealer who charges the customer five dollars a pound – the official price. Six hundred elephants a year are being killed, merely because the game laws cannot be enforced, and people want chessmen, or a new set of billiard balls.

Fourth, there are the status-killers, like the eagle chasers and the young car-borne bravados of Arabia.

Finally, and probably most important, are the inadequate game and conservation laws and the means of enforcing them. Social justice may appear to demand the equal and unlimited right to kill animals, but it does not seem much like natural justice if it results in the extermination of species. Conservation may mean complete protection, but not necessarily. In most cases it means proper control. The mistake so often made by the ill-informed and the sentimental is that they are quite unable to see the difference between controlled conservation and indiscriminate destruction.

In Africa, for instance, there would be no need to impose complete protection on a great many animals. In fact, if properly managed they could provide a very welcome protein addition to the peoples' diet. Many of the plains animals are, as it happens, far more thrifty and better-suited to the conditions than any European livestock. What is more, thousands of people from all over the world will travel to see the great herds in their natural surroundings.

These animals are in fact a vital economic asset to these countries, so long as they continue to exist.

Noah was commanded to build an ark and to take into

it a pair of every living creature to save them from the flood. Today a different kind of deluge threatens the earth's creatures and the World Wildlife Fund is the ark built by men and women and children throughout the world to give them a chance to survive the thoughtless actions of mankind.

The problem the Fund is trying to tackle is enormous and it needs money on the same scale. It involves educating people, influencing governments, enforcing laws, initiating ecological and biological research, conducting surveys and sometimes even buying land, or propagating threatened animal species in captivity, rather like Noah.

The problem in Africa is particularly acute, where the economics of the emerging countries are under very considerable strain as it is. It is not as if their leaders did not understand. For instance, Julius Nyerere, the first Prime Minister of independent Tanganyika, had this to say:

> *'The survival of our wild life is a matter of grave concern to all of us in Africa. These wild creatures, amid the wild places they inhabit, are not only important as a source of wonder and inspiration, but are an integral part of our natural resources and of our future livelihood and well-being. In accepting the trusteeship of our wildlife we solemnly declare that we will do everything in our power to make sure that our children's grandchildren will be able to enjoy this rich and precious inheritance. The conservation of wildlife and wild places calls for specialist knowledge: trained manpower, and money; and we look to other nations to co-operate in this important task, the success or failure of which not only affects the continent of Africa, but the rest of the world as well.'*

I believe we should do everything we can to encourage this enlightened approach.

Even so, the Fund cannot hope to succeed on its own. What is needed above all are people all over the world who understand the problem and really care about it. People with courage to see that the letter and the spirit of the conservation and game laws are obeyed and, where necessary, improved. People who care enough to bring up their children to have a proper respect and appreciation for wild animals.

Not just a few people here and there, but literally hundreds of thousands of ordinary people, as well as naturalists and sportsmen, game-wardens and zoologists, so that we shall be able to say with satisfaction that at least in this one endeavour mankind was able to correct its mistakes in time by a conscious and deliberate effort of will and generosity.

6th November 1962.
Speech at the British National Appeal Banquet of the World Wildlife Fund.
London.

This appeal has even more formidable problems to overcome. In the first place it has got to batter its way through the barrier of ignorance, indifference, emotion, and prejudice, to get the facts of the situation understood and appreciated far and wide. In the second place, the present situation is not brought about by any national disaster, a thing which Lord Mayors support almost immediately because they crash down upon people and animals without distinction. The unpalatable fact about this wildlife crisis is that it has been brought about by men. There is no getting away from it. For this disaster man, and man only, is responsible.

Perhaps the most difficult problem of all is to explain the basic purpose of WWF. As far as this country is concerned, this is probably even more difficult, because all the world knows only too well that the British have a 'thing' about animals. Whether in earnest or in jest, the subject is fraught with emotion. So you can judge how important I believe this appeal to be merely by the fact that I have dared to enter into these orders at all. The basic and the most urgent purpose of this fund is to help those species of animals which face extinction. It is not setting out to protect all animals from everything. It has no intention of campaigning against mouse-traps and fly-paper. Its function is to see that no other animal species goes the way of the dodo. Because the dodo, as you probably know, is a perfect example of the species of animal which has been totally exterminated. There is no living dodo left; there never will be another one. I'm quite certain that stuffed dodos and even partly burnt ones, which I think are the only ones left, may be absolutely fascinating to some people, but I can't really believe that they compare with the live article.

I freely confess that a few years ago I had no idea whatsoever that all sorts of wild animal species were dying out. I had no idea for instance, that since 1900 man has exterminated on an average one species every year. I'd even less idea that, unless something pretty drastic was done fairly quickly, another thousand species of vertebrate animals might become extinct within the next few years. But even knowing all this didn't make any difference, until I began to find out why so many species – not individual animals – are under sentence of extinction. After all, everybody knows that the mere process of evolution made the mammoth and the brontosaurus become extinct thousands of years ago. So what's all the present fuss about? Well, the difference is really quite simple. The cause of the present situation is not just the slow, natural process of evolution but the very rapid changes brought about by man himself. Man is the crux of the situation. It seems to me that if man is capable of causing animals to become extinct it must surely be his responsibility to see that he does not do so. The problem might be easier if we were doing all this on purpose. The trouble is that it is done all quite unintentionally, as if in a fit of absentmindedness. We may have little control over evolution, but we should be able to control our own even involuntary actions.

20th November 1962.
Address on Receiving Fellowship of the Australian Academy of Science.
Canberra.

Wonderful work in biology, zoology and comparative medicine is being done in many parts of the world. But the people who work in nature's laboratory, the wild places of this world, find themselves beyond the scientific fringe in more senses than one. Yet it is thanks to these careful investigators that the threat to wildlife in all its forms has been revealed. The crisis is pretty serious by any reckoning, but even so the full picture has not yet been filled in.

For instance the International Union for Conservation of Nature has evidence that at least a thousand species of animals are so rare, or are thought to be declining so rapidly, that they can reasonably be held to be threatened with extinction. Some twenty of them are in Australia including the Tasmanian wolf, Leadbeater's possum, the short-necked tortoise, the Australian night parrot and the noisy scrub-bird. The Union also estimates that at least ten Australian mammals have become extinct since they were first recorded. These lists are certainly not complete and much more information is needed about these subjects.

The fate of these animals is only part of the story; plants and insects are suffering in the same way. Australia in particular has a wonderfully rich heritage of plants and animals, many of them unique in the world. These living things have taken millions of years to develop, and only a detailed scientific knowledge of their existence can save many of them from extinction. The point is that all this is part of man's environment and if science loses interest in their future it will have walled itself up good and proper in a reinforced concrete tower.

Let me say quickly I don't think there is any chance of this happening here in Australia, and I hope very much that more countries will follow the example which this Academy is setting in this field. The attention which you have given to the fringe subjects such as the conservation of water resources, the grazing practices on high mountain country, the conservation of nature and the natural resources in general, and the establishment of national parks, is of the very greatest importance just in this period of history. I would only, and very diffidently, suggest one further subject for your attention. There are a great number of alarming reports of the effect of certain kinds of pesticides and herbicides on all living things right up to and including man himself.

I've seen some of these effects myself; whole areas where every living creature from small songbirds to foxes and hawks have been virtually wiped out, and where the survivors have become unable to breed. Chemistry has a great part to play in man's progress, but I'm sure it ought not to do so at the expense of man's health and environment. It isn't good enough to say that nothing can be proved conclusively; there mustn't even be any suspicion about it.

Equally, it is no good saying that the reports are exaggerated. This is just like saying that the danger of firearms is much exaggerated because not all murders are committed with firearms.

11th May 1982.
Speech to the Council for Environmental Conservation Conference.
London.

Having got this far, things become easier in the philosophical sense but a great deal more difficult in practical terms. The questions that have to be answered are:

1. *What species are under threat of extinction?*

The answer is gradually being built up by the Species Survival Commission of IUCN in its Red Data Books. The list is getting frighteningly long.

4th June 1982.
The Chancellor's Lecture, Salford University.

In order to get some idea of the problems faced by the conservation organizations, I think it might be an idea to divide endangered species into groups. There is no particular significance in the order which I have chosen. First of all, terrestrial plants – if you dig them up, cut them down, burn them or reclaim the land on which they exist – not only will they cease to reproduce and grow, but so will all the animal species that have come to be dependent on them and the area in which they grow. The tropical rain forests, for instance, harbour the largest number of species of any major habitat. The WWF has recently launched a world-wide campaign to tackle the issue of tropical rain forests.

Secondly, terrestrial animals. These come in two categories, the residents and those that migrate. Residents need habitats that can provide support and nourishment all the year round while the migratory species need to be able to move round depending on the seasons. From a practical conservation point of view, resident populations are largely national problems, whereas the conservation of migrants usually needs to be tackled internationally.

Thirdly, aerial animals. These also come as residents and migrants. Generally speaking, the migrants can move far greater distances, but they depend upon a string of resting and feeding places along their route. As a very large proportion of these migrants are either water or wading birds, the wetland habitats such as marshes, estuaries, lakes and mudflats are extremely important. As such areas usually include trees and bushes, they do almost as well for a number of the migratory and resident perching birds. The Ramsar Convention on the Protection of Wetlands of International Importance is one of the most important factors in the conservation of migratory birds.

Fourth, there are the aquatic animals and plants. Again, some are migratory and some are resident; but perhaps even more than terrestrial animals, aquatic animals tend to congregate in breeding and nursery areas before spreading out into the oceans. Consequently the disturbance of sometimes quite limited areas can affect a large number of species. The Waddensee, for instance, which runs along the north-west coasts of Denmark, Germany and the Netherlands, is a nursery area for most of the different species of fish in the North Sea.

You will, I hope, appreciate from this that the conservationist is confronted by the need to select certain land areas – including forests, mountain uplands, marshes, jungles and islands – that harbour species in danger of extinction. In some cases, such as the Campaign to Save the Tiger in India, the fact that the tiger is at the top of the food chain means that the areas given protection for the tiger also protect a great many other species at the same time. Further more, tigers are found in jungle swamps, open savannahs and in barren upland, so that the twelve national parks established in India have given protection to a very wide range of species in addition to tigers. The latest problem, strangely enough, is that with an increasing number of tigers in a country with a rapidly growing human population a higher proportion of tigers are becoming eaters of domestic stock and man.

11th May 1982.
Speech to the Council for Environmental Conservation Conference.
London.

In some cases, such as the whales, the answer – commercial exploitation – is fairly obvious. In other cases it is neither so obvious nor so convenient. Where human development projects, for instance, have the effect of eroding the natural habitat of one or several species, it is very difficult to arrive at an acceptable assessment of priorities or reasonable compromise.

There are so many instances of not necessarily recorded developments. In the south-east corner of Austria the water areas are there; but with the gradual encroachment of more and more agricultural activities, and irrigation, they can now grow crops that they couldn't grow before. There's a tremendous increase in vine growing, and the vines have to be treated with various chemicals; these are getting very close to the shallow lakes and, of course, there is a run-off. The run-off problem in agriculture generally is one of the most significant influences on water resources in the world.[1] (Second of course comes acid rain.)

3. Having established that a species is threatened and deduced the reason for the threat, the next question is to establish *what should or can be done about it*. The catch about this question is that the obvious answer is hardly ever the right one, and even if the right answer is found it does not mean that it is practically possible. IUCN is doing a splendid job answering this question.

4. And then the fourth question is, *how is all this going to be paid for?*

Development agencies throughout the world dispose of several billion pounds every year in financing development and aid projects throughout the world. The amount of money which is actually being invested in conservation is minimal. UNEP gets a small allocation and a part of that goes to IUCN. IUCN has to fund its own administration and its projects have to be funded to a large extent – something like 80 per cent – by money raised by WWF.

When you think that UNESCO gets an income of $300 million a year and WWF collects in the region of $10 million, you will see there is an imbalance in the amount of resources going into conservation and into other cultural activities. I should add that governments spend quite a lot of money on conservation projects and although UNESCO and UNEP are more concerned with the human environment there is a considerable overspill into pure nature conservation.

Operation Tiger is an example of the direct involvement of a government. WWF offered $1 million to the Indian Government to finance Operation Tiger, to which the latter contributed a further $8 million. The result has been eleven or twelve tiger reserves in India.

22nd November 1983.
Address to the Federation of Indian Chambers of Commerce and Industry,
and the Association of Members of Chambers of Commerce.
Delhi, India.

This has probably been the most successful major conservation programme with which WWF has been associated in its twenty-three-year history. There are now fifteen tiger reserves throughout India and the tiger population has risen from barely 1,500 to nearly 4,000. That is only part of the success story. The spin-off has been even more dramatic. Apart from giving all the other rare animals and plants in the reserves a chance to survive, the vegetation has increased and this has halted the soil erosion which in turn has resulted in clean, clear water in the rivers running out of the reserves, even in the dry season when many used to dry up. The buffer zones around the reserves are also recovering from over-exploitation and they are now supplying some of the needs of the villagers on a sustainable basis.

Positive conservation projects that set out to 'save' a threatened species or habitat only provide a part of the answer, although probably the more visible part. Prevention, or not doing something that might cause a threat, is far more effective. That is why the World Conservation

Strategy is so important. If governments, development agencies and developers generally followed the principles laid down in the strategy, most of the critical situations would not occur in the first place.

18th February 1981.
Address to the All-Party Conservation Committee.
London.

Some conservation enthusiasts seem to make an emotionally based distinction between 'pest' animals and what might be termed 'pet' animals. For instance, I strongly suspect that it would be easier to raise enthusiasm for the protection of the otter than for the adder. Yet in conservation terms they are both equally important. I also get the impression that some people find it difficult to see the difference between the death of individual animals and the extinction of a whole species. The important point is that provided a breeding population remains, and it has somewhere to live and breed, the species will survive. If, as in the sad case of one of the races of giant tortoise of the Galapagos, only one or two males remain alive, the species is doomed to become extinct. What no one can know for certain is which species are becoming extinct through natural causes, although it is usually pretty obvious which ones are becoming extinct through human progress.

People on the whole do not much like insects, and farmers are quite likely to become apoplectic about aphids. The eradication of mosquitoes by persistent chemicals in the campaign to control malaria produced some dramatic side-effects on the natural environment. Unfortunately, insects provide essential food for a mass of larger animals.

In this country partridges, for instance, depend on protein-rich insect food for the first fortnight of their existence. Aphicides mean higher yields for farmers but they also mean starvation for young partridges. However, there are all sorts of ordinary domestic products that eventually find their way into waterways and estuaries which are just as toxic to the insect food of other species and to the breeding areas of many fish. It was reported only recently that 850 birds died between August and November 1980 in the Mersey estuary and 2,400 the year before. At the moment there is no certain explanation.[2]

The strange thing is that it always seems to be those animals that do best which have the least appeal. For instance rooks, rats and crows always appear to be booming in spite of much discouragement, while woodpeckers, red squirrels and butterflies seem to have terrible difficulties holding their own. In the case of the red squirrel it seems to be unable to compete with the introduced grey squirrel.

In some cases there has been a dramatic revival of a species for no very obvious reason. Ten years ago there were virtually no wild geese anywhere on the Wash. Today there are several thousand pinkfoot. Only a few years ago it looked as if the Brent goose would disappear, but against all the odds it has made a splendid comeback. Others to reappear in this country are avocets and ospreys, but again the point is that it is their habitat that needs care and protection, particularly from curious humans, if the populations are to prosper.

There is even a chance that in ten years or so, it will be practically possible to produce clones of animals nearing extinction. A clone is a complete and identical replica of an animal grown from the genetic material in a cell of the parent animal.

Translocation of animals is now much more easily accomplished since the development of a gun capable of firing a tranquillizing dart, but of course it all depends on finding a suitable alternative location.

11th May 1982.
Speech to the Council for Environmental Conservation Conference.
London.

All conservation bodies need to be constantly on the alert to monitor and to report even the slightest changes in their particular speciality. And that is why it's so important for conservation bodies to keep in the closest possible touch with each other, because it's through this network that the vital information reaches the IUCN and appropriate action can be initiated.

As to the long-term prospects, they really depend on three things, the limitation of the human population, public support, and peace.

Public support depends on public knowledge and understanding of the whole conservation issue. The World Conservation Strategy, and, it is hoped, in due course the National Conservation Strategy, sets out the principles that have got to be exposed to the public and no one else can do this but the voluntary conservation organizations themselves.

Human conflict, whatever form it takes – terrorism, civil war, aggression, or international warfare – is the most directly destructive influence on nature and the natural environment. As it is so desperately wasteful, and in the first instance so stupid and unnecessary, it might seem easy to prevent. Sadly I have to say that while human nature remains as it is, conflict is bound to continue.

A very good example of this is the taskforce in the Falkland Island area which obviously has to protect itself against submarines. Unfortunately whales return an echo which is very similar to that of a submarine, and I can only assume that a number of them have been killed as a result. This is just one of those inevitable consequences of any form of conflict.

However, if the human population can be limited, and ultimately perhaps even reduced, there is hope that the cause of conflict might also be reduced, so that future generations can continue to live with consideration for all their fellow living beings and in harmony with the natural environment.

18th October 1984.
Keynote Speech to the World Wildlife Fund/Asahi Forum.
Tokyo.

The situation of the giant panda in western China illustrates virtually all the problems confronting the world of living nature. Unfortunately I have to say that all these problems derive from one basic source – the phenomenal success of one particular species – *Homo sapiens*.

For generations human communities existed in a general balance with the natural world. Occasionally it happened that one civilization or another became particularly successful and expanded much faster than others. In ancient times this happened to the Mayans in Central America, to the Hittites in Asia Minor, to the people of Mesopotamia and of the Indus Valley. In every case they consumed the raw materials, provided by their natural resources, faster than those resources could regenerate and the civilization collapsed. As a consequence most of those areas became deserts and have remained so ever since.

In modern times the differences are, firstly that the basic materials for industrial communities are minerals and other non-renewable resources, and secondly that the scientific and industrial revolutions have made it possible for the world's population to increase beyond anything known in history. It is now four times what it was 200 years ago and there is every chance that it will increase from over 4,000 million today to 6,000 million by the end of the century. This time when the resources run out the whole human complex is likely to collapse.

There is one very simple rule; it is that the planet earth can only sustain a certain volume of life. We live on a globe that cannot expand so that the more people inhabiting the earth, the less room there is for any other form of life. Just look around Tokyo. Apart from the human population how much other life manages to exist?

Look at China – the population today is about 1,000 million, roughly equivalent to the population of the whole world 200 years ago. As was absolutely inevitable, this huge increase has resulted in the demand for more food from more agricultural land; more natural resources, such as timber and fish; more pollution from human and industrial effluent; more soil erosion, and the consequent reduction in the space available for the populations of wild animals and plants.

The giant pandas used to roam in bamboo forests that stretched throughout the whole of western China and covered millions of square kilometres. Today, human encroachment and exploitation have reduced the forests to about 30,000 square kilometres. It is only due to their rarity and shyness that pandas have not suffered quite so seriously as other animals as a result of the commercial demand for their skins or as food. Not quite so seriously, but quite seriously enough.

Without taking moral and ethical requirements or emotional attitudes into consideration, there is no purely 'conservation' reason for prohibiting the exploitation of wild species for commercial or sporting purposes, provided such exploitation is limited by the ability of species to produce a sustainable surplus.

Conservation means the survival of species, and to achieve the conservation of species we need the help, support and involvement of all nations. It is the responsibility of the richer nations – such as Japan – to help the less wealthy nations to conserve their natural heritage.

Pandas also inevitably suffer from the other consequences of human encroachment; particularly disturbance, erosion and pollution. Pandas may be fortunate for the time being in that their bamboo forests are only affected by encroachment and the natural cycle of die-back and re-growth. The future is even bleaker for forest animals in other parts of the world which are affected by the more insidious menace of acid rain.

It may be comforting to imagine that it is only necessary to control the human influence on the survival of pandas, but the degradation of the environment cannot be put into reverse quite so easily. In fact many of the effects of human interference can never be reversed. In any case extinction is forever.

Similarly, it may seem that all is not lost while it is possible to breed pandas in captivity. All may not be lost, but is there really much point in maintaining a captive population if there is no prospect whatever of re-introducing them to their natural habitat because in the meanwhile it has simply disappeared?

The panda illustrates the real dilemma and the serious challenge to mankind. The fact is that this dilemma has to be resolved in our generation. If we in this generation do nothing to give the rest of the living world a chance to survive, we will be signing its death warrant. For those who prefer to be more concerned with human welfare and human survival, let me just say that the death of nature also means the death of mankind.

Trees and Plants

Extract from Foreword to 'Our Green and Living World: the Wisdom to Save it', Ayensu, Cambridge University Press, 1984.

The most important part of habitat is the tree and plant population. Animals cannot survive without them. This discovery leads in turn to the appreciation that plants are very important to the environment as a whole. They convert atmospheric carbon dioxide into plant material and release the oxygen that we have to breathe to stay alive. It hardly takes an expert to notice that modern industry and power stations are producing ever greater quantities of carbon dioxide just at the very moment that the earth's tree and plant cover is being eroded faster than at any time in history. The surplus of carbon dioxide is now forming a layer of gas in the atmosphere which tends to act like the glass in a greenhouse, it lets the sun in but it prevents the heat escaping. Plant destruction, unlike animal destruction, affects weather and climate, and if it continues unchecked it may eventually make human life impossible.

Plants have yet another useful property. Many of them are edible and while we may fondly believe that we can depend indefinitely on a very limited number of domestic species, the fact is that nature does not stand still and without the refreshment of the genes from wild species the common food plants might well decline in health and productivity.

Energy, food and building materials are not the only

things to disappear with the forests. Medicine will also suffer a very serious blow. There is no reason for ordinary people to know quite how dependent the pharmaceutical industry has become on plants for its raw materials. And that is long before the full medicinal potentiality of the plant kingdom has even been discovered. If the plants go, the medicines go.

Noah is said to have built an ark to rescue the animals from the flood. What the writer of Genesis fails to record is that Noah must also have collected the seeds of all the plants, because without them neither his animals nor his family could possibly have survived.

2nd March 1978
Opening of the Annual Conference of the Tree Council.
London.

I can think of a good many people rather more qualified than I to open this fifth annual conference, but I doubt whether the Tree Council could have found anyone with greater experience of formal tree planting. I have planted trees all over the world, I have even planted a Coco de Mer in the Seychelles and a Norfolk Pine in the Norfolk Islands; and several years ago I planted an apple tree in a church-yard in Grantham in the honour of Sir Isaac Newton. The next morning I discovered that it had disappeared. Efficient police work traced it to somebody's garden, and it was taken back and replanted. I am happy to be able to report that it has produced its first apple.

Whether all these trees survive or not is rather a different matter. Every time I plant one I have visions of the sickly saplings in various parts of the world struggling to stay alive. Some of the early ones which have survived are now nearly thirty years old and really quite respectable trees.

One of my latest efforts was to plant a tree at Windsor Great Park to start off the Tree Council's Jubilee Tree Planting Project. Of course not many of us are going to be around to see the new Queen Anne's Ride with its new avenue of trees in its prime, but we can at least enjoy the pleasant sensation of having done something useful for future generations. Apart from doing it myself, I have also caused, as it were, others to plant trees; and there is, I find, no greater satisfaction than looking at the results thirty years later.

Mind you, it does not always work. Disasters do occur, and there are times when I feel that my attempts are treated the way Moses persuaded God to treat the Egyptians. Mice, rabbits, hares, deer, birds, drought and beetles: I think these were only seven of the plagues visited upon my efforts in commercial forestry or to enhance the landscape. There are moments when even God himself seems to turn against these noble creatures of his.

In January this year the Head Forester at Sandringham told me, with justified satisfaction, that he had finally cleared up the mess caused by the gale in 1976. Two days later his pride was rudely shattered by another gale of equal ferocity, but this time from a different direction, which caught them up the skirts, as it were, and did no end of damage. The Head Forester is a Scot; which may account for this calvinistic rebuke on the part of the Almighty.

I am afraid these are part of the harsh facts of natural life. Facts which do not seem to be fully appreciated by some well-meaning and perhaps some rather sentimental urban dwellers. Trees are living things; they are born, they grow, they get diseases. They are subject to all sorts of natural disasters, and they get old and they die; they cannot be expected to last indefinitely, in the same way as ancient buildings can, no matter how much we love and cherish them. The best way to protect trees is to plant young ones to replace the old, which are bound to die sooner or later; and even this sounds a great deal easier in theory than it is in practice.

Each species of tree may be beautiful in itself; but that does not mean that they are equally appropriate in all circumstances. Apart from being able to do well in the soil and climate conditions, they also have to be right for the purpose, and I think there is nothing worse than those well-meant efforts called 'screenings' which turn out to be as much of a blot on the landscape as the thing being screened: almost as naïve as the sentimentalists or the people who believe that the landscape can be controlled by statute, as if legislation was like some sort of magic wand.

It was always my impression that it was King Canute who first demonstrated that there were limitations to the effectiveness of government decrees. I admit that government decisions sometimes have the effect they were intended to have; but more often than not they also have quite unexpected and frequently unintended consequences, and most of the changes to the landscape have taken place as a consequence of legislation intended to achieve quite some other purpose. Apart from anything else, it does not appear to be appreciated in some circles that trees take a long time to grow, whether they are planted for commercial or amenity reasons.

They are long-term benefits and if people are to invest in long-term benefits they need to have long-term confidence; and it is not just passing economic conditions or frequent changes in legislation about forestry alone that affect that sort of confidence. I believe that one of the most encouraging developments in recent years has been the growing public concern about conservation. But it is a funny thing about the British: we admire reformers and innovators, but we are always surprised by, and frequently very annoyed about the consequences of reform and innovation.

We admire the inventors of the railways, for instance; but there was violent opposition while they were being built. Yet the moment they started to go into decline, 'Save the Railways' societies started swelling up all over the place. We honour the engineers who designed and built Concorde, but the anti-Concorde lobby was and still is very powerful. I have no doubt at all that as soon as it looks like going out of service a 'Save the Concorde' society will be formed – if only to put it in a museum.

In the last 120 years or so, a lifetime of many trees, these conditions have changed completely. Industrial revolution, the population explosion, the growth of cities and the decline of villages, the mechanization of agriculture, the chemicalization of agriculture, and the whole structure of taxation, land tenure and population have changed out of all recognition. A hundred years ago 12 per cent of the population was engaged in forestry and agriculture; it is now down to 2.2 per cent. The reformers and the innovators have been, in fact, extremely successful; and predictably all sorts of organizations, voluntary and statutory, have sprung up to try to preserve the landscape and to prevent the inevitable consequences of their actions. It cannot succeed. You cannot stop the clock, let alone put it back; but just in case I am misunderstood, that is not to say that we should not try to prevent wanton destruction and inconsiderate exploitation. What we can do is to look to the future and to do what is possible within the constraints of contemporary social and economic conditions. There are a whole lot of things which it is within our power to achieve, in order to make the most of our environment, both urban and rural, and, particularly in that derelict planners' no-man's-land, where the two meet – in the vitally important but blighted green belt.

Conservation is for nature and wildlife and for that part of our environment which we admire, but there is no way of protecting a living landscape from change. A new landscape is inevitable and in my opinion we should be concentrating on those parts over which we have practical control. Such things as public land, Forestry Commission forest, parks, open spaces, motorways and railways, inner cities, river, rubbish tips, recreation areas, power lines, coast line and above all the urban-rural interface.

After all, more people are exposed more frequently to these neglected areas than have ever seen the beauty spots. There is so much we can do and the resources are so limited that it makes better sense to me to attack the black spots and the eyesores and to leave the people who live by the land to exercise their own taste and judgement. They are, after all, no less responsible or intelligent than urban members of committees and commissions, although of course they are much more sensitive to economic pressures. Let the foresters and the farmers get on with their jobs and they will do their best for the landscapes they know and live with and love. They have looked after it for a thousand years and I can see no reason why they should not be trusted to go on doing so within the contemporary social and economic constraints.

Down to Earth

18th February 1981.
Address to the All-Party Conservation Committee.
London.

Forestry is very often linked with agriculture, presumably because trees appear to grow like an agricultural crop. The only difference is that trees grow a great deal more slowly, so that the rotation can take anything from 60 to 200 years; and a plantation in this country has to be fenced against rabbits, hares and deer for the first twenty years at least. However, the main influence of progress on forestry is again machinery. Bigger, more powerful and more versatile machinery allows fewer men to cut and extract more trees from more difficult places than ever before. Much of the world's forestry operations take place in virgin forests, particularly in the great rain forests. Like the fish in the sea, these forests are looked upon as a natural resource just waiting to be exploited. Furthermore, the largest remaining natural forests happen to be in the under-developed countries, and who can blame them for cashing in on this source of wealth.

As you can imagine, the exploitation of natural forest areas inevitably has a considerable influence on all their animal and plant inhabitants. Some are resilient enough to survive, but the constant disturbance and the shrinking habitat lead to the slaughter of many species, which are anyway finding it difficult to survive.

It might be thought that replanting would repair the damage. It may well do so to a certain extent, but not unnaturally the only trees to be replanted are those that are commercially valuable. Furthermore, the usual practice is to replant in blocks of the same species of tree, while most natural forest is composed of a mixture of species, and this mixture is normally an effective protection against the spread of pests and diseases. When these break out in a

single species plantation they naturally have to be controlled by one means or another, with the consequent
side-effects on what wildlife is left.

13th October 1983.
Reply to Dr Boonsong Lekagul at a Dinner of the Thai Association for
the Conservation of Wildlife.
Bangkok.

Money is vital if we are to prevent a great many endangered species from dying out altogether, but the long-
term conservation of nature needs more than money. It
needs human understanding and self-restraint. It is easy
enough to say that development is vital for human needs
and it is equally easy to say that we cannot allow the wild
plants and animals of our world to disappear. The basic
problem about conservation of nature is that it needs to be
reconciled with development – or you can put it the other
way round, and say that development needs to be reconciled with conservation.

This is particularly true in the exploitation of renewable
natural resources; that is wild populations of plants and
animals. If you cut down a tree and another is growing in
its place, no damage is done and the resource will renew
itself forever. If you cut down a tree and the space where
it grew is taken away, that resource is gone forever. I am
sorry to have to say that in Thailand the area of replanted
forest in the last 40 years is 2,400 square kilometres, which
is less than the average deforestation (3,300 sq km from
1976 to 1980).

6th February 1985.
Lecture on Trade in Endangered Species.
Cambridge University.

The disaster from the conservation point of view is the country with natural forests. As might be expected such countries find it extremely difficult to refuse the lucrative offers of timber companies to extract the timber.

The combination of cutting forests, to meet the demands of world markets, and the more intensive cultivation of the land, to meet home demand, creates further problems. The weather patterns can be affected, producing drought conditions for man, beasts and plants alike. On the other hand if the rains continue as before they cause erosion of the soil, which in turn clogs up the rivers and silts up dams and estuaries. Once the soil is gone there is no chance of getting trees re-established. These effects are not peculiar to Africa or Asia. Inappropriate methods of cultivation have created dust bowls even in the United States. In well-meant attempts to improve agricultural output in countries suffering food shortage, governments encourage the use of chemical fertilizers, herbicides, fungicides and pesticides. Some of these chemicals are so toxic that their use has been banned in their countries of origin.

The general shrinkage of the areas previously available to wildlife is undoubtedly the major cause of the extinction of species. There is simply nowhere for them to live. A hundred years ago the Atlantic rain forest of Brazil covered thousands of square miles along the Atlantic coast. Today little more than about 10 per cent is left and its wild inhabitants have been reduced in proportion. The same is happening to the forests of Malaysia and Indonesia. The bamboo forests of western China are also rapidly disappearing and with them the habitat of the giant panda.

The picture is not entirely bleak. There is at least a

growing awareness among the governments of these countries that these forests and their wild inhabitants are renewable resources and, properly controlled, they could be exploited indefinitely. However, they have to balance the conservation of natural renewable resources for the benefit of future generations against the immediate and mounting economic and population pressures, and the outcome is by no means certain.

16th May 1968.
Speech at the Opening of the Forestry Building, Australian National University.
Canberra, Australia.

Research into forestry is therefore a vitally important activity. It is essential if we are to conserve, develop and manage important yet dwindling raw material. It is a determining factor in the reclamation of man-made deserts. It can help to find new uses for timber products. It can advance the whole concept of trees as a direct food source for various kinds of stock, and as I have suggested, it can make an immensely valuable contribution to the whole problem of the conservation of wild populations both plant and animal.

21st March 1984.
Speech at the Launch of the World Wildlife Fund/International Union for Conservation of Nature International Plants Conservation Programme.
Kew, Surrey.

The purpose of this meeting is to inaugurate the WWF/ IUCN International Plants Conservation Programme, so you can see that Kew is in fact a very appropriate place for it to take place.

The Plants Programme has two principal objects. The first is to draw the attention of as many people as possible and as many countries as possible, to the fact that the wild plants of our world are in just as great danger as the wild animals. In fact the disappearance of plants and forests is the immediate reason for the extinction of a great many animal species. I think it would be true to say that the world's human population is more directly dependent on plant than it is on animal life.

It is estimated that our world supports some 250,000 flowering plant species alone. Over 60 per cent of these are found in the tropical forests, and when the tropical forests go these plants go with them. In 1982, WWF/ IUCN launched a tropical forest conservation programme in an effort to contain the massive damage being done by short-sighted, unplanned and frequently unscrupulous exploitation of these primeval forests. But tropical forests are not the only ones at risk. In Germany an estimated 35 per cent of the trees are in a state of decline or death. In an article published recently in the *International Herald Tribune*, Robert Bruck, a plant pathologist at North Carolina State University, is quoted as having said that something very dramatic is happening very quickly to the forests of eastern United States. His studies have established that virtually no plant life is reproducing at the top of Mount Mitchell, the highest peak on the eastern seaboard, and this is leaving the once lush mountain top increasingly barren – a finding he described as 'scary'.

The tropical forest campaign has not solved the problem by a long way and fund raising for it will of course continue. The Plants Programme is really an extension of the Tropical Forest Campaign and will cover all the 25,000 plant species said to be in danger of extinction.

The success of the campaign will depend on getting the simple message across to the public in all parts of the world, that a great many useful, valuable and beautiful plants are in danger of extinction, unless drastic steps are taken as soon as possible to give them reasonable protection. In order to get this message across we need the interest and co-operation of the media, and we are very encouraged by the presence of so many of its representatives here at this meeting. With your wholehearted support there is a hope at least of slowing down the rate of destruction. Without it the work will of course go on, but the chances of making a significant impression are very slim.

The second purpose of the programme is to raise funds to pay for individual plant conservation projects. A great deal can be achieved by persuading people – from government ministers to peasants – not to act irresponsibly, but only by the expenditure of money on first aid and long-term conservation projects can there be any serious prospect of rescuing any of the plants in immediate danger of extinction.

Everyone has heard the expression 'dead as a dodo'. That was one animal species that became extinct some 200 years ago. Today something like 40,000 plant species could go the same way as the dodo by the middle of the next century, if we don't take some very determined action very soon. That is what this programme is all about.

14th October 1984.
Statement at the World Wildlife Fund Plants Campaign Press Conference.
Tokyo.

WWF and IUCN are partners in the campaign to ensure the survival of wild species in nature. WWF is the fund-raising partner and IUCN provides the expert knowledge. Together we seek to stimulate public awareness of the need for the conservation of nature and education about the natural world.

Among many other initiatives and projects, from time to time we generate publicity and fund-raising programmes associated with some particular aspect of conservation. We have had special campaigns for pandas in China, for tigers in India, for polar bears in the Arctic and for tropical forests. The current campaign is directed at drawing attention to the problems of the plant kingdom. The world would be a sorry place without animals but without plants it would be uninhabitable by men or animals. The oxygen we breathe in and the carbon dioxide we breathe out is re-cycled by green plants; most of our food is either directly or indirectly derived from plants; many drugs and medicines are derived from plants and all the beauty in our gardens and parks is provided by plants. And what would happen to the designers of kimonos?

It is easy to imagine that we have discovered or domesticated all the useful and beautiful plants in nature, but this is certainly not true. We are absolutely dependent on the genetic diversity in nature to ensure that our domesticated plants are able to resist diseases and maintain their productivity and so continue to supply our needs.

My experience of Japan is that people have a particular love for living plants. They have a traditional talent for the design of gardens and the arrangement of flowers.

This means working with nature. I believe this is only a short step to working *for* nature.

It may not seem like it, but the plants of this world are seriously threatened by such things as pollution, human encroachment, over-exploitation and soil erosion. It is not too late to prevent a disaster, but it will need a major worldwide effort.

Natural Habitats
and Genetic Resources

14th March 1973.
Speech at a Parliamentary Luncheon.
Canberra.

There is plenty of evidence that wildlife is being threatened. In broad terms, this threat is due to the rapidly increasing human population, with its consequent demands for more living space, more agricultural land, more industry and transport facilities, more resources and to the consequent pollution of the land, air and water.

The solution to the problem of the natural environment is not very difficult in principle, but it has some quite serious snags in practice. Setting aside wilderness areas in which the wild animals can live is the obvious answer. The trouble is that it is just those areas which are wanted for new agricultural land, for housing, for mineral and timber resources, for water storage and all sorts of other purposes. In addition, many of the areas are either already partly inhabited, or at least used in some parts of the world, by nomadic peoples.

There are, of course, many wild populations, particularly wild birds, which have existed together with human populations from time immemorial. Their problems are rather different. In many cases, things like pesticides, herbicides, drainage schemes and changes in the pattern of farming have either removed their food supply or their nesting possibilities. There is a further difficult problem, well known in Australia and New Zealand, and that is the effect of introduced wild species, or domestic species which have gone wild, upon the indigenous populations. In Australia, the rabbit, the buffalo and the camel are the most obvious examples.

The threat to the natural environment very quickly alerted people to the threat to their own, the human environment. After all, if fish and birds are being poisoned by polluted waters, it will be our turn next. If wild places are being threatened by increasing human population, what about places for human recreation?

17th May 1973.
Address to the Scottish Wildlife Trust.
Glasgow.

We all need to learn much more about what our country-side and wildlife can stand by way of human curiosity and disturbance. A free-for-all scramble without understanding or compromise between all the conflicting interests can only end in disaster.

People may well be anxious about the cost of conservation but at least they are aware that some compromise between all forms of development and the protection of the natural environment is necessary and reasonable. The really encouraging fact is how much can be achieved by sensible precautions against causing unnecessary damage, how quickly derelict land can be restored and reoccupied by wildlife and what great advantages there are to be gained by the proper management of wilderness areas, both for the enjoyment of people and the survival of wildlife. However, I believe we ought to look even further ahead. We know that people and wildlife can coexist, but only on certain terms.

The great safari parks of Africa have demonstrated that millions of people can enjoy wild nature if the whole thing is under proper and sensitive management. There have been some very successful imitation safari parks in this country on a miniature scale, but most of them are only glorified zoos showing animals which are not native to these islands. I believe Scotland has an opportunity to create something quite new in the way of a genuinely European wildlife area where only past and present indigenous forms of wildlife could exist under natural conditions and in such a way that they could be seen by large numbers of people.

The irony is that measures to protect particularly sensitive wilderness areas frequently have the effect of attracting more visitors. It would obviously be desirable, but probably not practical, to restrict entry to such areas to those who are prepared to join a particular organization. This would put them into a single 'communication group' and give them a proprietary interest in the area, and therefore make it possible to influence their behaviour.

18th February 1981.
Address to the All-Party Conservation Committee.
London.

As you can imagine, the exploitation of natural forest areas inevitably has a considerable influence on all their animal and plant inhabitants. Some are resilient enough to survive, but the constant disturbance and the shrinking habitat is equivalent to the slaughter of many species which are anyway finding it difficult to survive.

It might be thought that replanting would repair the damage. It may well do so to a certain extent, but not unnaturally the only trees to be replanted are those that are commercially valuable. Furthermore, the usual practice is to replant in blocks of the same species of tree, while most natural forest is composed of a mixture of species, and this mixture is normally an effective protection against the spread of pests and diseases. When these break out in a single species plantation they naturally have to be controlled by one means or another with the consequent side-effects on what wildlife is left.

Modern scientific methods have made it possible to learn a very great deal about the life-cycles, habitat needs, food and predation factors in a very large number of animal species. If there are still problems about rearing certain species in captivity in order to ensure their survival, we do at least know what could be done to give them a chance to survive in the wild. In many cases we know what factors are causing a certain species to be in danger of extinction, even if it is difficult to do anything about it.

19th May 1985.
Address to the Council Meeting of the World Wildlife Fund.
Divonne, France.

Since we met in Washington last year, I have had the opportunity to visit a number of National Organizations (that is apart from the United States and Canada). In Hong Kong, I heard about the very interesting co-operation that is developing between WWF-Hong Kong and the conservation organization in mainland China. I was very pleased to find that they were working closely together, particularly in connection with the protection of the coastal marshes which are so important for migrating bird species.

I was also asked to visit Algeria, Niger, Mali, Senegal, Gambia and Mauritania. Of these, only Algeria and Senegal had any effective National Parks or protected areas. All the other countries are in desperate need of such areas, both for the sake of their own resources as well as for the very large number of migratory birds that winter along the coastal mudflats and on the flood plains of the Niger and Senegal rivers.

4th June 1982.
The Chancellor's Lecture, Salford University.

At the other end of the scale there are reserves of as little as a few acres in this country set aside perhaps for just one rare orchid or a butterfly. The air is important as prevailing winds carry pollution very long distances. For instance, the sulphur emissions from tall factory and power station chimneys in this country are thought to be responsible for acid rain falling in Scandinavia. The unfortunate part about it is that these chimneys incorporate sophisticated scrubbing techniques designed to remove particulate matter and were especially built higher than usual with the very object of carrying the effluent clear of the surrounding population. It seems that the solution of one problem has merely created another.

The Victims

21st May 1984.
President's Address to the Council Meeting of the World Wildlife Fund International.
Washington DC.

Some people in Austria were not very pleased with me the other day when I pointed out that Austria had signed the Ramsar Convention and yet was proposing to destroy two internationally important wetland areas which the Government of Austria had itself designated under the convention. Contrary to what some rather over-excited commentators reported, I did not tell the Austrian Government what it should do about this problem. Neither did I suggest that a nuclear power station would be better than a dam and hydro-electric power station on the Danube. Those decisions are for the Austrians themselves to make. I am sorry if the Austrian authorities feel embarrassed by being reminded of their obligations under the Ramsar Convention but WWF International is part of the world conservation movement and I feel that attention must be drawn to such situations where necessary, without WWF in any way becoming involved in internal national affairs. I should add that the Vienna State Opera donated to WWF a handsome proportion of the proceeds of a performance of 'Aida' and, on the following evening – but not in the Opera House – there was a special performance of 'Cats' for the benefit of WWF – both well supported by 1001 members. There is undoubtedly much popular support for WWF and all it stands for in Austria.

3rd May 1984.
Statement at a World Wildlife Fund Press Conference.
Vienna.

No visitor can fail to be impressed by Austria's natural landscape. The high mountains, forests, rivers and lakes are also the homes of many wild animals and plants. Some of the animals are resident all the year round, others, particularly birds, are migratory and only come to Austria at certain times of the year. The eastern part of the country is exceptionally rich in wild plant and animal species as this area is at the eastern limit of the normal range of western European species and the western limit of the range of many east European and Asiatic species.

Austria is indeed a fortunate country and Austrians should be happy and proud to have such a rich natural heritage within their territory.

On this occasion I can only speak as a visitor and an admirer, but I am a very interested visitor. I am President of World Wildlife Fund International which raises more money for the conservation of nature worldwide than any other voluntary organization. I am interested in Austria for two important reasons.

Everyone in Austria must have heard of the Lange Lacke by now. It is an area of great natural beauty, which everyone can see, but it is also an extremely important area of wetland. Apart from many unique resident species of animals and plants, the area provides a refuge for very large numbers of migratory waterfowl. During the last twenty years WWF International and WWF-Austria have paid 18 million schillings in rent in order to ensure the protection of the area from agricultural development and indiscriminate hunting, mostly by foreigners who pay the landowners for the privilege. This contribution was made on the understanding that the area would be given proper statutory protection. This promise has not been kept.

Let me emphasize that the money spent by WWF on the protection of the Lange Lacke is all derived from voluntary donations. They come from over one million regular subscribers all over the world, from young and old, rich and poor, all united in their concern for the conservation of nature.

They give us their money to achieve the survival of wild plants and animals. What am I to tell them about the money we have spent in Austria? How am I going to explain that their money has been wasted as we have failed to achieve long-term protection of the Lange Lacke area, and that in all probability wine-growers, fish farmers and hunters will take over the area next year?

As far as hunting is concerned, I was very surprised to learn that hunting and the protection of animals is a matter for the provincial governments. Consequently there is no standard national hunting or animal protection legislation in Austria. Even more surprising is that the close season for game animals and the lists of protected species are different in each province and in many cases these lists do not include species on the international list of species in danger of extinction.

The second reason I am interested in Austria is this. IUCN, WWF, UNEP and other international organizations spent many years struggling to introduce an international convention giving special protection to wetland habitats, including those which are particularly important for migratory waterfowl. The convention was eventually adopted at a meeting at Ramsar in Iran in 1971. The Austria Federal Government acceded to the Convention in

1982. There are now 35 contracting parties to the Wetland Convention and international interest in this treaty is growing rapidly.

The Convention provides for general obligations relating to the conservation of all wetlands throughout the territory of the Contracting Parties as well as for specific obligations for wetland sites designated by each Party and added to the List of Wetlands of International Importance.

Under the Convention Austria has nominated five sites, including the Lange Lacke and the riverine forest along the Danube, and it has therefore made a solemn and public international undertaking to provide these vitally important areas with significant protection. If the terms and spirit of the Convention had been properly implemented there would be no threats to the future of either the Lange Lacke or the Danube riverine forests, and I would probably not be speaking to you here today.

How can we possibly go to the poor countries in Africa, Asia and Latin America and ask them to sign and implement the Ramsar Convention when a rich European country, having accepted the Convention, is apparently quite content to ignore its terms?

I can only add that I hope I may be forgiven for the things I have said this morning. I felt I had to say them out of my regard for Austria and the people of Austria and out of my commitment to the conservation of what is left of the natural world.

As you have seen in the slide presentation, other important international treaties, specifically the Washington and Bern conventions, have been ratified by Austria, but apparently they too are not being enforced.

I am sorry to have to say it but I believe that Austria is

in grave danger of tarnishing her reputation within the community of nations.

That is a matter for Austrians, but it also reflects on the credibility of the whole international conservation movement.

Tropical Rain Forests

3rd February 1986.
Address to the European Management Forum Foundation Symposium.
Davos.

The exploitation of natural forests only becomes a conservation problem when the remaining areas become too small to support their full range of wild inhabitants, or if the disturbance caused by the extraction operations drives out rare species.

This is particularly critical with tropical rain forests since they contain something like 85 per cent of all known natural species of plant and animal. The dreadful fact is that these forests are disappearing by an area the size of Austria every year. The trouble is that once cut down they cannot be regenerated. This is because the forest, the soil and the rain are mutually dependent on each other. When the tree cover goes, the soil is liable to be washed away and the pattern of the rainfall is likely to be affected. It is for this same reason that clearing certain areas of rain forests for cultivation of other crops, or in order to establish single species plantations, does not succeed.

In fact if you look around you will notice that the main desert areas of this world each sustained an advanced civilization until the demand for resources, particularly of timber, became greater than the rate at which they could be replaced. The Hittite Empire for instance in Asia Minor; in Mesopotamia, in Persia, in the Indus Valley, in North Africa. They are all still denuded of trees and suffer to a greater or lesser degree from erosion and desertification.

Where it can be done successfully, the plantation of forests as a source of raw materials is obviously preferable to letting the land become a desert. However there are some dangers. Massive plantations of exotic species are completely useless to the native fauna and, in most cases, the remaining native flora cannot survive in such plantations. Furthermore, exotic species may well have a different way of using the available water, and this may affect an area far greater than the plantation itself.

14th October 1983.
Speech at the President's Banquet.
Kuala Lumpur.

Forty years ago Malaysia had an exceptionally rich heritage of wildlife on land and in its seas. Twenty years ago perceptive observers began to notice that the situation was changing. They noticed the first signs of the effects of population growth, exploitation of natural resources, erosion and pollution. Then eleven years ago the situation became serious enough for WWF-Malaysia to be founded and today, largely thanks to the efforts of WWF-Malaysia, there is a large and growing public awareness of conservation problems and anxiety about the future.

This pattern is not unique to Malaysia. In recent years nearly all the countries in the world's rain forest belt have experienced the same sequence of events. It is this anxiety about the future of the tropical rain forests that stimulated the International Union for Conservation of Nature and Natural Resources and the World Wildlife Fund to launch the special appeal for a comprehensive rain forest conservation programme.

I think it is important to bear in mind that this conservation programme is not just an emotional and unconsidered reaction to the threatened extinction of wild animals and plant species. It is rationally based on the World Conservation Strategy, which was worked out after a great deal of research and consultation by IUCN, UNEP and WWF.

The strategy defines three objectives – the maintenance of essential ecological processes, the preservation of genetic diversity and – most significantly for the rain forest countries – the sustainable utilization of species and ecosystems. Every farmer and cultivator understands the principle of sustainable yield. They know that they have to conserve their resource whether it is cattle or rubber trees if they are to expect an income in the following year. Unfortunately, this principle does not always appear to be understood by those who are responsible for the resources of the natural rain forest.

From the point of view of wildlife conservation, the progressive exploitation of the rain forest is a disaster because something like 85 per cent of all living species of plants and animals depend on the existence of these forests for their survival. But the threat to the survival of this wildlife is only one of the consequences of over-exploitation. Far more serious, from the human point of view, are the economic consequences. Farmers know about not eating their seed corn; economists ought to know the consequences of living on capital – you end up begging the IMF for assistance.

I was in Bangkok yesterday and amongst other things I discovered that the total acreage of forestry land replanted in the last 40 years was less than the average acreage cut in a single year. Quite apart from the implication that the Thai people are exploiting the very valuable national capital resource represented by the natural forests instead of relying on a steady income, there are even more serious consequences.

For example, let me quote from a paper prepared by WWF–Malaysia in June this year:

> '*Soil eroded from logged slopes piles up behind dams or flows out to sea, turning the shore waters a murky brown. Deep-draught ships bypass Port Klang because silt washed from unprotected land under development in the Kland basin has reduced the depth in the Port's North Channel from 11 metres to 9.4. Magnificent coral reefs are being destroyed by fish bombing, coral collectors, and siltation. Perhaps half of Malaysia's species of plants and animals are threatened with extinction as their lowland forest homes are cleared for other uses . . .*
>
> *. . . Such unfortunate results of development could be greatly reduced if conservation needs were incorporated into development planning. This is the goal of conservation strategies being prepared by the World Wildlife Fund – Malaysia. Since the individual states have control over land matters in Malaysia, these strategies are being formulated state-by-state.*'

Even that is not the end of the problem. A recent study on 'Precipitation and Water Re-Cycling in Tropical Rain Forests' by the IUCN Commission on Ecology reveals a whole series of other dangerous consequences. For instance, land converted from natural tropical forest to some other productive use does not absorb the rainfall at the same rate. As a result 'even if the rainfall is there much of the water would not remain for return to the atmosphere'. It then goes on to say that 'if there is a reduction in water returned to the atmosphere this will result in a reduction in cloud cover and a corresponding increase in light intensity and heat'. It estimates that the solar energy reaching the soil surface of a cleared area is something like 25 times greater than in the forest and that the soil temperature rises about 10°C, making it even more vulnerable to erosion when the rains come.

The study concludes that soil erosion has the major impact on water recycling through its long-term effects on soil productivity. Once erosion has started it can lead to virtually irreversible degradation of soil and cover vegetation. Loss of soil even from forest land converted to cultivation is significantly greater.

Add to all this the loss of potential new medicines, pharmaceuticals, insecticides, the diminution of the genetic pool for domestic fruits and cereals, the loss to irrigation, hydro-electric and marine resources through siltation, and to the supply of clean water for industry, agriculture and the growing human population. The economic consequences of the over-exploitation of natural rain forests for short-term gains become only too apparent.

The study further concludes that deforestation of large areas of tropical rain forest would tend to reduce the rainfall on forest areas downwind, which could drastically change the nature of adjacent forest. These effects are local, but reduced cloud cover has global implications. To quote again: 'What is known is that cloud formation provides a major form of heat transfer, and is a critical element in global heat balance. Consequently there would be a potentially important alteration in global climate'.

So what may have started out as a concern about threats to the survival of wildlife turns out to be a concern for the long-term economic security of the people, and ultimately for the survival of all life on earth.

The next three speeches deal with the problem of conservation in Madagascar. WWF first became involved in the campaign to arrest the process of destruction, erosion and depletion taking place as a result of the felling of tropical forests, in 1981. Although all three speeches in this sequence were made within a very short space of time, it is possible to discern a certain change of tone from one occasion to the next as the gravity of the situation becomes increasingly apparent.

10th June 1985.
Speech at a Fund-Raising Dinner of the World Wildlife Fund-UK.
London.

With the world's human population still exploding, although, thankfully, not quite as fast as it was a few years ago, and with the consequent demand for natural resources, such as land, water, timber, wildlife and wild-life products, and with pollution and erosion adding to the general degradation of the natural environment, I think I need hardly spell out to the present company the vital need for measures to prevent the current crisis becoming a future disaster.

I say 'measures' rather glibly; it is obviously a great deal more complicated than that. Some of you have made donations to the special appeal for Madagascar – and others have contributed to the Masai Mara appeal, so I am sure you have read about the special problems of these two very important areas. The problem for WWF is to convert those funds into successful and significant conservation achievements.

80 per cent of the tropical forest of Madagascar has

already gone, and with it the habitat of any number of unique species of plants and animals. The destruction of the Masai Mara is just as serious. I need hardly say that no amount of money can replace the lost forest, but well-selected and carefully planned projects might be able to slow down, if not entirely prevent, any further irresponsible exploitation.

4th November 1985.
Address at the National Conservation Strategy Conference.
Madagascar.

This is the first opportunity I have had to visit Madagascar and I would like to say what a great honour and pleasure it is to be invited to take part in this most important conference. Anyone with the slightest interest in natural history knows that this island contains a unique and fascinating flora and fauna.

I would like to start by offering the Malgache government the most sincere congratulations on behalf of the whole international conservation community, on two counts:

In the first place, for being the first to develop, and to officially proclaim, a national conservation strategy based on the principles of the World Conservation Strategy.

Secondly, for taking the initiative in organizing this conference to discuss ways and means of implementing the National Conservation Strategy.

As an introduction to the theme of this conference I can do no better than to quote from an article which appeared in the *Midi Madagaskari* of 3 October this year:

'Beaucoup de ressources naturelles sont malades, atteintes dans leurs structures écologiques; les problèmes sont connus depuis longtemps. La déforestation s'accroît, parfois jusqu'à créer des zones entièrement dénudées, donnant au panorama un visage de tristesse, voire de désolation. L'érosion augmente, et, progressivement, les éléments riches de la terre s'en vont pour ne laisser que des sols souvent incultes.

Les examples ne manquent pas autour de nous concernant la dégradation des ressources naturelles. Mais face à cette situation, une initiative de taille est en préparation, car il semblerait que l'heure n'est plus à la passivité mais à l'action. Que faire pour sauvegarder le patrimoine malgache avant que les dégâts ne soient irrémédiables?'

'Many natural resources are ailing, their ecological structures are damaged. We've known about the problem for a long time. Deforestation is on the increase, sometimes to the extent of creating completely denuded areas, rendering the landscape sad and desolate. Erosion is likewise increasing, and the earth's own wealth is disappearing, often leaving land quite incapable of supporting cultivation.

Examples of the abuse of natural resources are all around us. But we are about to take appropriate measures to deal with this situation, for it seems that the time has come to shake off our passivity and take some positive action. How are we to safeguard Madagascan heritage before the damage becomes irreversible?'

That, dear colleagues, is the challenge that faces us during the next few days. It is a daunting challenge but is one that the international conservation community must not fail to meet. It will be a major test of our sincerity and commitment and the eyes of many other developing countries will be upon us.

Since everyone attending this conference is fully aware of the threats to the well-being of the world's natural environment and of the serious over-exploitation of the world's natural resources, I do not propose to go over that familiar ground on this occasion. In any case we are not concerned here with abstract arguments, but with the hard practicalities of implementing an agreed strategy. Everyone attending this conference has some part to play in this process but I would like to address my remarks particularly to those who are representing the international conservation community.

I believe it is most important to be clear about one thing. This conference was called at the initiative of the Malgache government. The ultimate responsibility for the implementation of the National Conservation Strategy rests with the government and people of Madagascar. As representatives of the international organizations we are not here to tell the Malgache authorities what they should be doing, we are here to offer our support, our technical advice and our co-operation.

If we are to do that effectively it seems to me to be vital that whatever assistance our respective organizations are able to offer should be properly co-ordinated. Let me say right away that I have nothing but admiration for the motives of the international organizations and for the dedication and technical competence of all who work for them. However, I must also say that I have come across altogether too many instances of lack of co-ordination, conflicting and overlapping projects and the understandable, but short-sighted, desire to gain exclusive merit and recognition.

If I could assume that we were all of a religious disposition I would suggest that in matters relating to the conservation of nature it is better to lay up a store of merit with the Creator of Nature in heaven than to seek honour and publicity here on earth. But that may be straining human nature too far.

I believe that the cause of conservation is too urgent and too important for our all too slender resources to be wasted through jealousy and pride. So let us begin by committing ourselves wholeheartedly to our common aim: the conservation of the natural environment and resources of Madagascar for the future benefit of its people and for all life on this still beautiful island.

In the words of the national anthem:

Ry Tanindrazanay malala o	*O beloved land of our ancestors*
Irinay mba hitahiana anao	*We desire that you may be blessed*
Ka ilay nahary izao tontolo izao	*That He who created the world may be*
No fototra ijoraon'ny satanao.	*The upholder of your life and dignity.*

As you know, the conference programme includes the formation of four specialist 'workshops'. Incidentally, while I realize full well that it is a very awkward subject, I believe that it would be quite unrealistic to exclude any discussion of the problem of the pressures exerted by a growing human population at the conference dedicated to the long-term conservation of nature and natural resources. It would be like denying that the moon had any influence on the rise and fall of the tide.

That is why I would propose that this conference be re-convened in about five years from now to review progress and to chart the course for the next five years.

Meanwhile I can only urge you to make full use of the opportunities afforded by this conference to map out a bold and imaginative programme designed to implement the National Conservation Strategy quickly, simply and, it is to be hoped, cost-effectively.

7th November 1985.
Remarks to the Plenary Session of the National Conservation Strategy
Conference.
Madagascar.

I have been in Madagascar for five days, but sadly I have to leave tomorrow. No doubt I should have attended the technical sessions, but instead I was able to visit the north, west and south coasts of an island that retains places of spectacular beauty. This vast experience naturally qualifies me as an expert on every aspect of life in Madagascar. However, you will be relieved to hear that in spite of this I do not propose to trouble you with my views on the future development of Madagascar.

In fact I am very hesitant about saying anything on this occasion. I believe in the dictum that a little knowledge is a dangerous thing. All I would like to do is to make some comments based on my experience of many other countries.

I hope I may be forgiven for saying that for an island that is so heavily dependent on forest and water resources, I find it difficult to understand how it is possible that the country has been almost totally denuded of forests and that the water regime has been so heavily polluted by soil erosion. It also surprises me that the co-relation between forest destruction and the conservation of rainfall seems to have been ignored. I find it difficult to escape the impression of a country intent on committing suicide.

The situation may be new for Madagascar but it is not

unknown in the history of human communities. The fact is that most of the great human civilizations of antiquity succeeded in destroying their habitats by the same means. Mesopotamia, Persia, the Indus Valley, the Hittites of Asia Minor, North Africa, Greece and Central America, all succumbed to the three great destroyers; first, growing prosperity leading to rapid population increase; second, over-exploitation of forest resources for fuel and building materials, leading to soil erosion and the reduction of rainfall; and third, over-intensive cultivation of the soil leading to the decline in fertility.

I do not want to be discouraging, but the natural environment and the natural resources of those areas have never fully recovered.

I believe that Madagascar can escape that fate, but it will entail some drastic and, in some cases, quite painful decisions.

I do not want to minimize the task which faces the government. It may well be true that under a democratic system the government is elected by popular choice, but the fact remains that the business of government is never popular. This is true whatever the structure of the constitution or the ideological complexion of the governing party. It is an unfortunate fact that government is not a popular activity with those who are being governed.

I think it would also be true to say that legislation is only as good as its enforcement.

It seems to me that the lesson we all have had to learn in recent years is that economic development can no longer be the single and absolute goal of all government policies. It is becoming increasingly obvious that a tolerable environment, social, spiritual, physical and natural, is essential to human welfare.

This conference is concerned primarily with the natural

environment and the conservation of natural resources, but it cannot be said too often that conservation is a part of the development process as a whole and not an alternative to it. The issues before this conference therefore concern all the bilateral and multi-lateral aid agencies, as well as all the private and voluntary foundations. I believe that the only way we can meet our obligations in Madagascar is by recognizing that we are all part of the same process and that we must work together to achieve the same end.

I believe that this conference has helped all the extra-national agencies to gain a better understanding of their responsibilities and opportunities. I hope it has also helped the Malgache authorities to appreciate better what we are trying to achieve.

This broad concept of conservation also poses a difficult challenge to the government. It needs to have a clear policy, rational legislation and the will and the means to carry both into effect. This is essential if the aid agencies are to have the confidence to make significant investments in their particular fields of activity.

Apart from the designation of various categories of protected areas and the reinforcement of their management system, legislation and enforcement needs to cover the control of the exploitation of wild species of terrestrial and maritime plants and animals for whatever purpose, be it for hunting, or as a source of food, for commercial purposes, for tourism, or for export. Needless to say, the control of the current wave of pyromania must have a high priority. None of the measures will be popular, but in most cases I believe it should be possible to arrange matters so that it is in the interests of the local people to abide by the rules.

Without their more or less willing co-operation there is

little hope of success. However, this will require a considerable programme of education and enlightenment.

After all the horror stories I have heard and some of the very disturbing sights I have seen, it would be easy to despair of being able to achieve any significant success in the limited time available. But there is one characteristic that is shared by everyone concerned with the conservation of nature, and that is almost unlimited optimism.

I would like to congratulate the Minister and the Department of Waters, Forests and Animal Production and, indeed, the whole Malgache government on the organization of this vitally important conference. It has done wonders for our optimism and I am sure that it has raised the confidence and morale of the many people in this country who are passionately concerned to ensure that this island retains its unique character and can continue to justify the title 'The paradise of the Indian Ocean'.

Minerals and Fuels

27th November 1973.
Speech at the Conference on Fuel and the Environment.
Eastbourne.

Fuel and the environment have been causing serious problems for mankind ever since the earliest times. Our difficulties are nothing new, they are just a bit more sophisticated. There are many parts of the world which at one time supported flourishing civilizations but which are now useless deserts or barely support goat-herding nomads at the lowest level of human existence. We know that those areas once had great forests and rich agricultural land but we also know that, like all living organisms, human communities grow in numbers to consume the resources available.

The forests disappeared as they were exploited for fuel and building material, while the fertility of the soil was destroyed by overgrazing and over-cultivation. These ancient civilizations collapsed because they could not deal with their energy crisis and because they destroyed the natural environment upon which they depended. I dare-say, of course, that they were also plagued by waste disposal problems, pollution – particularly of water sup-plies – soil erosion, urban renewal difficulties and, in the last resort, by wars.

Eventual equilibrium is established and maintained when the rate of regeneration is balanced against the population numbers controlled by climate, availability of

260

minimum levels of food and fuel, and by disease. In a mild climate human life can exist at a very much lower standard than in a harsh climate, which makes it virtually imposs- ible for regeneration in a harsh climate to achieve a level high enough to sustain anything better than a subsistence nomadic existence.

In many parts of the world the whole system has been drastically modified by the development of technology, which has made it possible to exploit resources hitherto unusable. Perhaps the most significant was the develop- ment of new sources of energy, which at last gave independence from wood as the major structural and energy resource.

Technology, therefore, opened a completely new store- house of resources and of course, the inevitable happened. As they became industrialized, populations exploded in one country after another. Medical science helped popula- tions to grow even faster than they would have done anyway. As if that were not enough, the economists added their little bit by suggesting that labour meant wealth and with that characteristic leap of the imagination, for which economic theorists should be famous, they propounded that more people also equalled more consumption and, therefore, even more industry and wealth.

In this country we have been riding the crest of a wave for about 150 years. The population has been growing steadily to consume the resources of coal and iron ore which we were fortunate to find in the ground. We made a fortune from these resources in the nineteenth century, just as the oil producing areas of the Middle East are growing rich on their resources now. The exploitation of our resources gave us a lead in technical know-how, which made it possible for us to sustain the growth in population and standards of living long after the most easily available resources were used up.

But as far as the natural environment is concerned, it has taken a very severe hammering, first from the development of technology and the production of energy in all its forms, and, secondly, from a growing population with ever-increasing standards of consumption.

This vast increase in the population alone has made a considerable impact on the environment. Where, in addition, the average rate of consumption of resources and water and the production of waste per person has increased by something like 100 per cent in the same period, the impact is even more noticeable.

The first signs of anxiety appeared many years ago, but it is really in the last decade that a great many people have begun to notice what was happening. Ironically, pollution and the exploitation of resources were identified as the major causes of the degradation of the environment, and that just at the moment when resources were beginning to get a bit thin anyway, when the demand for energy was growing faster than ever, and worst of all, when the less developed countries were just beginning to enjoy the fruits of technology. Furthermore, as the populations of these less developed countries increase, so the exportable surplus of their agricultural products and eventually, of course, of their other resources is decreased.

It does not require a great stretch of the imagination to realize that if resources become scarce and demand continues to rise, prices are liable to go up. At this precise moment people concerned with the environment are very reasonably demanding that levels of pollution should be reduced and the exploitation of resources should be more carefully controlled. Desirable as they are, it is no good pretending that these demands will not increase costs to the consumer still further. We are indeed facing a classic situation from which only a co-operative effort can possibly extricate us.

I think the conservationists need to know more about the practical problems and alternatives of meeting the forecast energy requirements in these islands, while the energy industries need to know more about the actual and the threatened impact of their industries on the environment. It is worth remembering that the energy sector comprises the country's largest capital investment in industrial processes, with an annual turnover of £1,000 million and 700,000 people employed. Every household in the land is a customer for at least one of its products. Furthermore we cannot contemplate a halt to the improvement in the standards of living of the people of this country who are less well off.

This is going to require more horsepower available for people at work, and more therms for household use of all kinds. This will have to come from more power stations and more fuel to feed them, whether it be coal, oil, gas, nuclear or any other source which may be developed meanwhile. These stations will have to be sited somewhere, and faced with the inevitable we must use everything science and technology has to offer to reduce their impact on the environment.

It is, therefore, rather more important than usual to ensure that expenditure for environmental or amenity reasons is justified by a measurable or significant improvement in the protection of the health, home, factory, crops or amenity of the consumer, or of what remains of our wildlife on land or in the waters.

Any discussion of the impact of the energy industries on the environment should take place against a background of exact facts and figures. But facts and figures are not the whole story. We face the far more difficult task of trying to define the sort of environment in which we want to live. It is bound to be a compromise, because there is a limit to the material sacrifices which people are prepared to make simply for some abstract concept of conservation. It is a bit easier to define the amenities which people can appreciate for their own enjoyment. It is much less easy to define conditions under which the rest of the living world should be allowed to exist. These things are extremely difficult to quantify so that conservation is almost always on the defensive.

The ideal would be to say in advance exactly what needs to be preserved or protected. This can be done in some cases, but more frequently the need to protect only arises in response to a specific threat. Either way we need the most exact estimates possible of the costs of protecting these amenities and of creating or preserving these conditions. Unless all these cards are put on the table it will be quite impossible to make any sensible assessment of the real problems which face us, or to estimate some sort of priority in seeking their solution.

29th November 1973.
Speech at the Conference on Fuel and the Environment.
Eastbourne.

As you know, this Conference was conceived before the present artificial energy crisis came upon us,[3] so I was naturally a bit anxious that it might be overshadowed by other considerations. I think it is a remarkable tribute to authors of papers that the crisis has not made any of their contributions irrelevant. Indeed, the crisis has merely served to emphasize all the points which they made, even if not everyone agrees with them.

My principal anxiety stems from the fact that I came to the conclusion long ago that it is a mistake to talk about solutions before the problems have been identified. I am not at all certain that we have properly identified all the problems which the extraction, processing, conversion and distribution of fuel create for the environment. Furthermore, I doubt very much whether it is possible to establish a priority among the problems which have been identified, and I doubt very much whether we, all of us here, would arrive at the same priorities anyway.

The impact of fuel on the environment is intimately bound up with the whole problem of our national energy needs and this is in itself a vast subject. It is important to the environment because the most efficient use of fuel resources is probably the single most effective way of protecting the environment, and it could, I suppose, be argued that the present energy situation is providing a very effective inducement towards a much more efficient use of fuels. I forget who it was who said that the threat of death powerfully concentrates the mind.

At first sight, it would seem that all we need to do is stop degradation, but that is only half the story. It is equally important to give positive encouragement to develop along what we hope are the right lines. For instance, it is no good simply forbidding the tipping of waste. We must make it a matter of self-interest and profit to treat waste in a sensible way. Therefore, I think that we should try to develop a more enterprising and a more realistic approach to legislation and economic intervention.

This Conference has demonstrated yet again that it is possible for people with different attitudes to meet together and to put their points of view calmly and fairly and to listen to other opinions. It is quite apparent to me that where disagreement exists it is due to sincerely held beliefs, and where criticism is made it is offered in a constructive sense.

The trouble is that there are many people who simply believe that God has made a better job of the landscape than man, either as a farmer, architect or engineer, can ever hope to do. They reluctantly accept that developments for human convenience are necessary, but nothing will convince them that they can ever compare with nature in beauty. This is a matter of opinion and it is much more difficult to reconcile opinions than to settle on the facts.

I am therefore glad to say that a joint working party has already been set up under the impartial auspices of the RSA, including representatives of this Institute and the Council for Environmental Conservation, to keep all these issues under review and to allow the exchange of opinions and anxieties.

So I would suggest that we must take all reasonable steps to use every source of fuel and energy as efficiently as possible. This really rephrases recommendation No. 9 in the Institute's publication:

> *'Measures to use energy in its various forms more efficiently should be instigated at once, in particular methods for the more efficient conversion of heat energy into electricity should be developed and the waste heat generated put to use wherever possible.'*

I find this publication particularly valuable, and I believe that all our fuel and energy industries, and government departments responsible for them, would do well to read it. If they have not got time to read it all, I suggest they go through the conclusions and recommendations which are very thoughtfully printed at the beginning of the report.

I would just like to draw attention to one or two of these recommendations. For instance, No. 5 says:

> '*Coal will have an increased importance in the fossil fuel market during the next two decades provided that prices are kept within reasonable bounds*'; and No. 7: '*Research in diffusion power should be substantially increased*'; and No. 10: '*Well-established technology for the efficient use of fuel should be promulgated in industry and techniques for insulation applied and encouraged wherever fuel is burned.*'

The efficient use of fuel resources is vital, but it is not the only criterion. For instance, it is quite obvious that actual damage, and the risk of potential damage, through breakdowns and accidents is a very significant factor indeed. Then again, the generation of electricity through hydro-electric schemes does not pollute, but it certainly makes an entirely disproportionate impact on the natural environment and usually in its most sensitive areas.

Any attempt to deal with the whole spectrum of fuel and energy is going to be an immense challenge, and yet I suspect that many of our difficulties derive from the way in which we treat fuels and energy industries as separate entities. Indeed, the one overwhelming impression I have gained from this Conference is that we must deal with energy as a whole. Dividing it up into arbitrary categories only succeeds in confusing and distorting the issues, forcing decisions to be made, which may make sense in isolation, but which are patent nonsense in relation to the energy problem as a whole.

Recommendation No. 14 says:

> '*An energy commission should be set up to oversee the co-ordinated use of energy in the United Kingdom.*'

I think we must find some way in which to control and integrate all our fuel and energy industries and to organize the search for and the development of new sources of energy.

However, practical considerations alone are not really enough. I think there is another factor which is equally important in creating a satisfactory energy/environment balance. I would describe it as the intellectual factor. This can be further subdivided into knowledge and attitude.

It is quite obvious that if we are to make any headway in the more efficient production and use of energy and in the search for and the development of new sources of energy, we are going to need a sufficient number of the appropriate scientists and technologists. My impression is that there may well not be enough of these people to put these immensely important social needs into practice. So I think we need to interest young people in the technologies for the energy industries.

Knowledge is essential, but attitude is almost equally important. It stands to reason that it is impossible to have an opinion if you are unaware that a problem exists. It could be argued that there is only one satisfactory technical solution and provided the designer balances all the factors in precisely the right way, the ideal result will be achieved. However, one of the most important factors is the consequence and impact of the design on the environment and assessment of consequences and impact are to a large extent a matter of opinion. I suppose opinion should really be based on knowledge and a responsible attitude, but it can be based on ignorance and prejudice and this can cut both ways. Knowledge, someone said, is power, but right decisions cannot be taken if the public is either directly opposed to them or even if it is apathetic. We must therefore see to it that the public is informed so that it will not be in direct opposition to the measures necessary to protect it from its own avarice.

As far as energy/environment problems are concerned there are amenity, social, and economic, as well as environmental costs, benefits and risks to be taken into account, and this implies that judgement has to be exercised. This means, for instance, that if you believe that the long-term national interest is best served by the best rate of economic growth, accepting reasonable risks and at the lowest reasonable costs, then one set of decisions will follow. On the other hand, if you feel that a clean environment, the best amenities and the conservation of wildlife are more important than any risks, and the benefits are well worth the extra costs, then obviously a different set of decisions will follow. I would therefore point to the need to develop a much wider and much more lively discussion about the ethics and the moralities of environmental conservation. Legislation and the deliberate adjustment of the economic environment in which the fuel and energy industries operate through the manipulation of taxes, subsidies, investment inducements and so on, are the means by which future development is influenced.

So my final suggestion is simply to urge that we do all we can to maintain and develop the lines of communication which have been opened between the fuel and energy industries and those who are concerned about, or responsible for, the protection of our environment.

Down to Earth

26th April 1983.
Address to the Fellowship of Engineering.
London.

There can be no doubt that technologies change social and cultural patterns, but then, for example, so do crimes or wealth. However, it is worth bearing in mind that technologies are not developed with the express purpose of changing society or culture. The primary object is to meet perceived practical human needs. Vastly improved standards of transport and communications, public health and hygiene, housing and household gadgets, inevitably change ways of life. All these can raise material standards of living, and they certainly make it possible to increase the number of human inhabitants of this earth. There is, however, no evidence to suggest that they improve the quality of human behaviour or stimulate greater artistic talents.

Quite apart from the social and cultural consequences of modern technology, there is another area that is very significantly affected by technologies, and which in turn influences the living population of the world. Modern technologies have created a growing demand for the earth's resources, and they have also developed the means to acquire those resources at an ever-increasing rate. And in the long run – that is if there is to be a long run – common sense suggests that demand will have to be balanced against the sustainable availability of renewable resources. In that sense the success of modern technology poses a very important challenge to human ingenuity and an ever greater challenge to the present generation for the future of all life on earth.

I do not think that any discussion about modern technology can ignore what is certainly the most important challenge of modern technology to mankind: namely the development of the generation of power from nuclear reactors and of nuclear weapons. Both these products of technology pose baffling dilemmas. Evidence suggests that conventional power stations, together with some of the industries they supply, plus vehicle emissions, are mainly responsible for the acid rain which is destroying forests and killing life in rivers and lakes throughout the northern latitudes. Nuclear power stations may pose other problems, but they do not produce acid rain. Then again, all the evidence points to the successful deterrent effect of nuclear weapons. Although they do not stop small wars or the invasion by stronger powers of their weaker neighbours, they have prevented escalation, and they certainly appear to have discouraged armed conflict between East and West in Europe. Yet many people still seem fervently to believe that wars are created by weapons. The trouble is that any weapon capable of killing is dangerous the moment it gets into the hands of anyone with the intention of using it. For nearly a hundred years Britain had a naval fleet more powerful than those of the rest of the world put together, but it was not called upon to go to war until 1914. What is known to the Jewish people as the Holocaust was perpetrated without the use of any military weapons at all. More people have been killed by motor-cars or by terrorism than by bombs dropped in war.

Most people know that the destructive power of nuclear weapons is vastly, almost immeasurably, greater than that of conventional weapons. Therefore in all logic there is really no point in having any more of these weapons than the bare minimum to provide a credible deterrent. What really matter are the scruples of their possessors; the character of those individuals with the ultimate power to unleash them. People are far more dangerous than inanimate objects.

Many years ago Albert Einstein said that nuclear power had changed everything, and he added significantly 'except our way of thinking'. It is tempting to suggest that nuclear weapons are the ultimate social and cultural challenge of modern technology, but it would not be quite accurate. The challenge is not to such abstract concepts as society or culture. The challenge is directly to our human nature and to the way we think and the way we use our brains. The question is whether the threat of cataclysmic disaster can possibly bring those traditional origins of conflict, human greed, ambition and good intentions, under some sort of rational restraint and control.

V

CONCLUSION

With all the evidence available, it is difficult to avoid the conclusion that the future for this planet does not look very bright – to put it optimistically. The pessimist would say that it is doomed to be destroyed by one species of its own inhabitants. The difficulty is that few, if any, people in positions of political authority or responsibility have ever felt able to take a long-term view. I am sure that many of them appreciate perfectly well that the world is heading for a very difficult time, but voters have always been more concerned with their immediate problems. Furthermore, there is money to be made out of the exploitation of natural resources, which gives market economists and the prophets of development powerful arguments against taking a long-term view.

Conservation also suffers from another disadvantage. It has a lot of dedicated and knowledgeable supporters, but it has failed to make much impression on public opinion in general. I suspect that one reason for this is that anything to do with nature and natural processes is beyond the comprehension of the majority of the population, which lives in towns and cities. They are largely deaf to arguments about what might happen to future generations, and they are certainly not impressed by generalizations about such things as the growing world population or the exploitation of tropical forests which it is beyond their ability to regenerate.

The conservation movement as a whole is putting out a

very great deal of information, and is doing its best to argue the case for care and restraint; but it seems to be missing the target. The message does not seem to be getting through to 'the man in the street' or, more pertinently, to the men and women in government offices, aid agencies, education, the professions and, most important of all, the millions working in fields and forests. Neither is it getting through in a way that enlists personal commitment and a sense of moral obligation. Unless, and until, public opinion can be aroused in support of the conservation of nature, there is very little hope of making any significant headway. Therefore, it seems to me that there is a need to think of other means of attracting public attention. It was this concept which was largely responsible for organizing the World Wildlife Fund's 25th anniversary celebrations at Assisi.

The trouble seems to be that the rather selfish, anthropocentric, scientific and economic arguments are altogether too remote, and the issues far beyond the ordinary person's immediate preoccupations. The tendency is for people to simplify and personalize the issues into being kind to animals and having concern for the trees and plants in their immediate vicinity.

Fortunately, humans are not entirely governed by practical considerations. Attitudes are influenced by ideals, by principles, by convictions, and particularly by religious faith. Consequently, if the conservation of the natural system could be made into a matter of conviction, rather than being simply a practical matter of self-interest, there might be a chance of attracting support from a much wider constituency.

This possibility is strengthened by the fact that most, if not all, religions allow for some measure of divine intervention in the creation of the world and in the operation of the natural system. Therefore, if God is in nature, nature itself becomes divine, and from that point it becomes reasonable to argue that reverence for God and nature implies a responsibility not to harm it, not just for our own selfish interests, but also as a duty to the Creator. As the whole of the world's living system is inter-related and interdependent, and since mankind is now the world's dominant species, this responsibility and duty has become all the more urgent.

The experience at Assisi seems to have proved that this approach can be effective.

The Moral Imperative

27th July 1986.
Speech at the World Wildlife Fund's 25th Anniversary Conference.
Assisi.

One of the things which has struck me during this
conference is that we are confronted with a whole string
of dilemmas, awkward dilemmas. Take, for instance, the
problem of the short term and the long term; the advantages of short-term planning and the long-term problems
to which it gives rise; and these apply in all areas: industry,
politics and ethics.

Then there is the problem of private and institutional
interest in conflict with the public interest. We've heard
about the difficulties that governments have; we've heard
about the problem of private gain and public loss; we've
heard about the dilemma of altruism and ego, or anthro-
pocentricity. One of the speakers said, for instance, that
you can't expect somebody to care for an elephant just for
the sake of the elephant. Well, possibly not. But what are
we doing caring about whales? Very few people ever see
them and yet, for some reason or other, we *do* care for
whales – or at least a lot of us do – so there must be an
element of altruism in this attitude. It is not entirely
egocentric.

Then we have the problem of reason and emotion. We
can argue that we have scientific reasons; we do have
scientific discoveries. We have all sorts of reasonable
arguments and yet, in the end, half the things we do and

277

half the decisions we make are decided by emotional attitudes.

We have the problem, or the dilemma, of individual will and of how to convert it into public will. We heard about the difficulty of putting pressure on governments through uniting individual wills, so that public opinion can be formed out of a whole lot of individual opinions.

There is the problem of materialism against – I don't know what the opposite would be – emotionalism? We know that in many ways materialism is leading us up a blind alley, but what is the answer?

Then there is the dilemma of local problems as opposed to global problems. People can understand their local problems – they may well deal with them – but they don't understand that they are part of the global problem. Can you actually, really, personally and individually conceive of a global problem in a way that allows you to respond to it?

We have the dilemma of consumerism and conservation. We are all consumers in our way, yet we profess to be conservationists as well.

There is the dilemma which confronts the whole movement: are we going to act on the basis of confrontation or persuasion? What seems to me to have become very evident from our last session is that getting the message across depends very much on understanding human nature, and that we've got to adapt to the target audience.

Apart from these dilemmas, I would just like to mention one or two of the ideas that emerged which struck me as particularly interesting. I was interested in the concept of the eco-social contract. It seemed to me to embody the idea that you can bring the influence of conservation to bear on economic thought. Out of that emerges the associated idea of natural economy as opposed to money economy.

Another very interesting point was brought out by the reference to the cost of inaction; it's a concept which I think can be very useful, and I hope you will take it home with you and scratch your heads about it, because I think that it's something that one can present to the people who don't quite understand the message of conservation.

I was particularly struck by the values that seem to have emerged from religion, myths, folklore and taboos as expressions of global consciousness – referred to by Doctor Karan Singh – which are also means of conveying concepts in a way that is understood and which lead to these concepts being accepted as limitations on behaviour. This seems to be engaging, as it were, the right side of the brain – you heard about the great influence that taboos have on the way people behave.

We talked about the reverence for nature or, as I would prefer, the reverence for the natural system. Of course the difficulty lies in defining the meaning of the word 'reverence'. It seems to me that it is the acceptance that we are *part of* the system, even though we may have a decisive influence over it. Reverence may be desirable, but I'm afraid the reality is that our attitudes are governed by self-interest, or possibly an emotional commitment.

A point to remember, when we are trying to project the message, is that damage to the environment is done largely through ignorance and not through malice. I think this is important, because it's no good accusing somebody of being malicious. It's quite different to say, 'Look, I don't think you understand the problem.' People have all too many answers, but they have not discovered what the problem is yet.

Then there is the whole idea of the reaction of governments to public opinion: the problem of governments acting in what the individuals know to be the right way, only to be faced with the absence of public support. There is the other side of that coin. I suspect that when governments choose to send out messages to their public, such messages are received with a certain amount of suspicion. People have been governed for many, many generations and they are basically rather suspicious of messages from governments. They always suspect that they are sent out for either political or ideological reasons, and not for any altruistic reasons. I think a very important point to remember about governments is that they have a responsibility for looking after the public interest.

Also, and this is very important, they have to set the rules for the game. Somebody suggested that there has to be individual freedom. That is very important, but, if you come to think of it, in the game of football there are rules which all the players stick to, and which umpires make sure are implemented. That doesn't inhibit either the individual or the team talent. Provided you stick to the rules, there is ample opportunity for the development of individual talent, and even for team talent; and I think that setting rules for the game is what we want governments to do.

It seems to me that the idea that mixed messages are reaching governments is a very serious problem. It arises because they are being sent contradictory messages from so many local interests. I don't want to denigrate local interests in any way, for these are extremely important. I don't want to argue with them, but I do feel that if we are going to send contradictory messages, then we are going to be divided and ruled rather than have any influence on the way we are ruled.

Conclusion

Another interesting point is the idea that nature is a wasteful system, and that science can develop much more efficient systems by improving on nature.

Finally, the point made by Doctor Karan Singh about convergence. We have talked about conservation from a number of different points of view, and they have all tended to converge together. Whether it's the scientific, the economic, the commercial or the industrial, the political, the academic or the ethical, they all converge on the problem of the conservation of nature. We know that all life is interdependent, and I think it is now obvious that this includes all human activities. One of the most important lessons is that the promotion of conservation is a matter of understanding human nature.

24th November 1983.
Address to a World Wildlife Fund Dinner.
Bombay.

The last, and I believe the most important, answer is the moral imperative. There may be a lot of demonstrable practical reasons for conservation, but you have to believe that it is also right as opposed to wrong, and convinced that it is good as opposed to bad, for its own sake. Only a commitment to this altruistic, objective, indeed religious attitude is capable of uniting and inspiring people of all kinds and all interests to grapple with the problems that mankind has created for the natural world. Indeed, I suggest that conservation is the only issue that is truly international, inter-denominational, inter-ideological and inter-racial.

The moral imperative is recognized by all the great religions. In the Hebrew book of Genesis for instance,

God says, 'Let man have dominion over the fish of the sea and over the birds of the air and over the cattle and over all the earth and over every creeping thing that creeps upon the earth.' By dominion, there is little doubt that He meant 'have responsibility for'. I cannot believe that He meant 'exploit them to satisfy your greed'. Genesis also records that after Adam had eaten the fruit of the tree of knowledge God said, 'the man has become one of us knowing good and evil'.

The Hindu poets and the sacred legends of India tell much the same story. It is said the Brahma makes the flora of the earth, the trees, the flowers and the herbs the dwelling place of Indra.

There is the legend of Siva, the deity of the Himalayas, who persuaded the heavenly river Ganges to come down to earth. But to prevent the torrent shattering the earth, he spread his hair in the form of the forests to break the force of the river and to prevent the soil being washed away. Concern for soil erosion is nothing new. Indeed, the Emperor Ashok produced the first conservation strategy for India 2,300 years ago.

The Vedic poems are full of references to conservation. For instance, 'Whatsoever I dig from thee, Earth, may it have quick growth again! Oh purifier, may we not injure thy vitals or thy heart.' And again, 'May sweet to us be the night and sweet the dawns; sweet the dust of the earth, sweet be our father the sky above us. For one who lives according to Eternal Law the winds are full of sweetness, the rivers pour sweets, so may the plants be full of sweetness.' They also affirm that the deities are equally concerned with animals and that 'the woods belong to the birds'.

Krishna says, 'Under my presiding, nature generates all things, animate and inanimate and by this instrumentation the world functions.' And he continues, 'For if I did not do my work, these worlds would fall into ruin. I would become the creator of chaos and would destroy these people.'

Perhaps most telling of all are the references in the Vedic poems to the Kali epoch when men will indulge in greedy and senseless exploitation of nature. The poet was right, we are living in the Kali epoch today.

So you can see that far from being a newly invented, self-centred, European, middle-class, capitalist campaign, in India at least, the conservation of nature has been taught by the deities for centuries and runs as a distinctive thread through the whole rich tapestry of her religious philosophy and legend. No one can be left in any doubt that the spiritual leaders believed very firmly that the species *Homo sapiens* has a responsibility for the care of all the living species which share this planet Earth with us, and that it is morally right and good to ensure we do not cause their extinction.

LIST OF SPEECHES
AND WRITINGS

from which extracts have been included in this book

the National Council of Social
Service. London. (p. 98)

1972

24th April 1972. Speech to Open
the New Lecture Hall at Chester
Zoological Gardens. (p. 187)

1973

14th March 1973. Speech at a
Parliamentary Luncheon.
Canberra. (p. 236)

17th May 1973. Address to the
Scottish Wildlife Trust. City
Chambers, Glasgow. (pp. 112,
237)

23rd May 1973. Address at the
Annual General Meeting of the
Zoological Society of London.
(p. 189)

16th July 1973. Address at the
Salford University Degree
Ceremony. (p. 146)

23rd November 1973. The 4th
Jane Hodge Memorial Lecture,
The Institute of Science and
Technology. Cardiff. (pp. 89,
180)

27th November 1973. Speech at
the Conference on Fuel and the
Environment. Congress Theatre,
Eastbourne. (p. 260)

29th November 1973. Speech at
the Conference on Fuel and the
Environment. Congress Theatre,
Eastbourne. (p. 264)

1974

8th May 1974. Welcome to the
Members of a Symposium
Organized by 'The 1001: A

Nature Trust'. London Zoo.
(p. 191)

1977

26th February 1977. Speech at the
Dinner of the World Wildlife
Fund. Wellington, New Zealand.
(p. 127)

10th March 1977. Conference of
the Capital Cities Lords Mayor.
Brisbane. (p. 94)

1978

2nd March 1978. Opening of the
Annual Conference of the Tree
Council. RIBA, London. (pp. 94,
223)

15th March 1978. Presidential
Address to the School Natural
Science Society. (p. 38)

1980

1st October 1980. The Fairfield
Osborne Lecture. New York.
(pp. 65, 84, 103, 119, 127, 131,
148)

1981

18th February 1981. Address to
the All-Party Conservation
Committee (pp. 78, 95, 132, 147,
179, 182, 215, 228, 238)

27th May 1981. Presidential
Speech to the 20th Anniversary
Reception of the World Wildlife
Fund. Wembley. (p. 52)

1982

11th May 1982. Speech to the
Council for Environmental
Conservation Conference.

Zoological Gardens, London.
(pp. 30, 199, 210, 212, 217)

27th May 1982. Reply to the
President of the British Property
Federation. London. (p. 96)

4th June 1982. The Chancellor's
Lecture, Salford University.
(pp. 68, 86, 93, 95, 105, 121, 129,
132, 149, 183, 210, 240)

21st September 1982. Address to
the World Affairs Council. Los
Angeles. (p. 122)

1983

9th March 1983. Speech to the
Vancouver Canadian Club.
(pp. 128, 200)

26th April 1983. Address to the
Fellowship of Engineering.
London. (p. 270)

1st July 1983. Address on
Receiving Honorary Degree from
the University of Western
Ontario. Canada. (pp. 154, 193)

13th October 1983. Reply to Dr
Boonsong Lekagul at a Dinner of
the Thai Association for the
Conservation of Wildlife.
Bangkok. (p. 229)

14th October 1983. Speech at the
President's Banquet. Kuala
Lumpur. (p. 247)

15th November 1983. Address to
the Bangladesh Federation of
Chambers of Commerce and
Industry. Dhaka. (p. 79)

22nd November 1983. Address to
the Federation of Indian
Chambers of Commerce and
Industry and the Association of
Members of Chambers of
Commerce. Delhi, India. (p. 214)

24th November 1983. Address to
a World Wildlife Fund Dinner.
Bombay. (p. 281)

14th December 1983. Speech at
the Margaret Pyke Memorial
Trust Dinner. Commonwealth
Institute, London. (p. 151)

1984

21st March 1984. Speech at the
Launch of the World Wildlife
Fund/International Union for
Conservation of Nature
International Plants Conservation
Programme. Royal Botanic
Gardens, Kew, Surrey. (p. 231)

3rd May 1984. Statement at a
World Wildlife Fund Press
Conference. Vienna. (p. 242)

21st May 1984. President's
Address to the Council Meeting
of the World Wildlife Fund
International. Washington DC.
(p. 241)

31st May 1984. Introduction to
the Zoological Society of London
Symposium. (p. 123)

14th October 1984. Statement at
the World Wildlife Fund Plants
Campaign Press Conference.
Tokyo. (p. 234)

18th October 1984. Keynote
Speech to the World Wildlife
Fund/Asahi Forum. Tokyo.
(p. 218)

15th November 1984. Speech at a
Fund-Raising Dinner of the World
Wildlife Fund-UK. Fishmonger's
Hall, London. (p. 124)

Extract from 'Men, Machines and
Sacred Cows', published in 1984

by Hamish Hamilton, London.
(pp. 82, 168)

Extract from an Article in 'The Observer', London, 1984. (p. 91)

Extract from Foreword to 'Our Green and Living World: The Wisdom to Save It', Ayensu, Cambridge University Press, 1984. (p. 222)

1985

6th February 1985. Lecture on Trade in Endangered Species. Cambridge University. (pp. 113, 130, 230)

19th May 1985. Address to the Council Meeting of the World Wildlife Fund. Divonne, France. (pp. 89, 169, 239)

20th May 1985. Reply to Mr Anders Wijkman at the Council Meeting of the World Wildlife Fund. Divonne, France. (p. 171)

10th June 1985. Speech at a Fund-Raising Dinner of the World Wildlife Fund-UK. London. (p. 251)

4th November 1985. Address at the National Conservation Strategy Conference. Madagascar. (p. 252)

7th November 1985. Remarks to the Plenary Session of the National Conservation Strategy Conference. Madagascar. (p. 256)

1986

3rd February 1986. Address to the European Management Forum Foundation Symposium. Davos. (pp. 66, 108, 124, 246)

20th March 1986. Speech at the Launch of the World Wildlife Fund-UK's 'Planet Protection '86'. Institute of Civil Engineers, London. (p. 125)

30th April 1986. Lecture to the Royal Society of Arts. Royal Society of Arts, London. (pp. 81, 110)

27th July 1986. Speech at the World Wildlife Fund's 25th Anniversary Conference. Assisi. (p. 277)

14th November 1986. Lecture to the European Council of International Schools. Montreux, Switzerland. (pp. 17, 35)

1987

11th March 1987. Address to the Joint Meeting of the All-Party Group on Population and Development and the All-Party Conservation Committee. London. (pp. 87, 139)

Extract from an Article in 'The Shooting Life', London, 1987. (p. 184)

NOTES TO THE TEXT

1.   *The Greenhouse Effect*

In a greenhouse the panes of glass allow the sun's rays to pass through but trap some of the infra-red radiation. This reflects back from inside and blocks convection, thus heating the interior.

The earth's atmosphere has an analogous effect. Sunlight passes through it with little transfer of energy and is largely absorbed by the surface of the earth, which it heats. Part of that heat energy is then radiated back to the atmosphere in the form of infra-red long waves, a large proportion of which are absorbed by the carbon dioxide and water vapour in the atmosphere, resulting in an increase in the earth's temperature.

The increase in carbon dioxide caused by the burning of fossil fuels (coal, oil and natural gas) and the destruction of trees, which absorb carbon dioxide through their foliage, may intensify this effect and induce major climate changes which could even mean the rapid melting of the polar ice-caps. Before the Industrial Revolution the amount of carbon dioxide in the atmosphere was about 275–285 parts per million. By 1980 it was 338 parts per million and the proportion is still rising.

2.   *The Green Revolution*

The Green Revolution has nothing to do with the politically active ecological groups that we now know as the Green Parties. It was the term coined to describe the introduction of high-yielding seeds and modern western agricultural techniques in the developing countries of the Third World.

Down to Earth

It was a technological 'revolution' not a social one, and was led by the developed nations not by the indigenous populations. They have often gained little from it, and sometimes suffered as a direct result, while the beneficiaries have been the multinational corporations.

3. ## Trofim Denisovich Lysenko

Lysenko (1897–1976) was a Russian agronomist who dominated official biological theory under Stalin. He gained prominence by his revival of the technique of vernalization – interrupting the rest period of seeds shed in the autumn. The seeds are immersed in water which is then frozen. The effect is to speed up germination of winter-sown wheat so that even spring-sown crops mature before the autumn frosts. He claimed that an organism could be changed by altering its environment and that acquired characteristics could be passed on to later generations.

As a result of Lysenko's attacks the geneticist N. I. Vavilov was arrested in 1940 and exiled to Siberia. Lysenko's continued opposition to Mendelian genetics made it impossible to teach the chromosome theory in the USSR from 1948 to 1964, when the government withdrew its support from Lysenko, although he was allowed to retain his academic posts.

4. ## Sir Grafton Elliot Smith

Elliot Smith (1871–1937), born in Grafton, New South Wales, was an anthropologist and anatomist who led many expeditions in the Nile Valley. Through pupils, who included Raymond Dart, he was involved in discoveries of prehistoric man in Africa and China. From his comparative anatomical studies he suggested that man was descended from a tree-living, ape-like creature. He also presented the theory that all human civilizations had developed from the spread of a single original culture in Egypt.

5. ## The World Wildlife Fund and The International Union for Conservation of Nature and Natural Resources

Set up in 1961 by naturalists and others concerned for the future of the world's wildlife, WWF is now the largest world-wide nature conservation organization. Based in Switzerland, it has 24 national affiliates and associated organizations in five continents.

WWF aims to create critical awareness of threats to the environment and to generate and attract, on a world-wide basis, the strongest possible moral and financial support for safeguarding the living world and to convert such support into action based on scientific priorities.

IUCN was founded in 1948, thanks partly to the efforts of Sir Julian Huxley, then Director General of the United Nations Educational, Scientific and Cultural Organization (UNESCO). Until 1956 it was known as the International Union for the Protection of Nature (IUPN). It consists of a network of governments and non-governmental organizations, scientists and other conservation experts, joined together to promote the protection and sustainable use of living resources.

II EXPLOITATION OF THE NATURAL SYSTEM   pp. 61–133

1. *The Groundnuts Scheme*

In Britain during the late 1940s few single topics gave politicians and comedians as much to talk about as the Groundnuts Scheme, which became a byword for official waste and mismanagement.

Inspired by the knowledge that there was a considerable shortage of edible fats in the postwar world, the British government conceived a plan to both make up the shortfall and aid colonial development. The East African colony of Tanganyika was selected as the place for an immense project to grow groundnuts (peanuts).

Administration of the project was given to the Overseas Food Corporation (OFC) under Sir Leslie Plummer's chairmanship. Experts poured into Kongwa and other areas, the bush was bulldozed, a new town was built and the rural Africans surrounded by the latest European machines and technology. But, in January 1951, after an outlay of £6.5 million the scheme was abandoned.

Among the reasons given to the House of Commons

Public Accounts Committee for the failure was that normal commercial 'considerations' had been set aside for the sake of speed, that the ground–clearing machinery was unsuitable and lacked not only spare parts but even a method of acquiring them, that the land and climate proved less favourable than the feasibility study had suggested. The Committee also concluded that there was a 'lack of organization' by the Food Corporation and found its accounts unsatisfactory.

In fact, the scheme was incredibly badly prepared. Although it was known that several private farmers had lost large sums in tropical farming schemes, neither the Colonial Office nor the OFC seem to have taken much account of the nature of the soil, the climate or the tropical pests they might encounter. Sir Leslie Plummer, the OFC Chairman, resigned in 1951.

2. *The Gezira Scheme*

This major gravity–flow irrigation scheme in the land between the Blue Nile and the White Nile, in Sudan, forms the largest farm in the world under one management. It has turned an arid and desolate land into a prosperous green landscape, 12 per cent of the country's cultivated area, making a major contribution to the national income.

3. *Acid Rain*

Acid rain is only the most publicized result of irresponsible air pollution which could be prevented if proper precautions were taken. Dioxan, for instance, a highly toxic, insoluble compound used as a solvent for acetates, accidentally released with tragic effects in the Seveso disaster in Italy, has been identified as responsible for stillbirths and deformity in animals and sickness in people in Britain. No explosion or single release has been responsible: Dioxan can be produced in the routine combustion of waste materials, notably PVC, or the combination of chlorine with lignin (which is present in all woody substances and most paper). Incinerators at local authority or hospital garbage disposal units can accidentally create it. Careful control of temperature during combustion and measures to prevent emission into the air are necessary. The obvious solution is to fit efficient 'scrubbers', devices to filter and clean emissions before release, to all such incinerators and filters – but at present they are not compulsory equipment.

4. *The Body Shop*

Body Shop International plc is a manufacturing, wholesaling and retailing operation producing skin and hair care preparations. Their first shop was opened in Brighton in 1976. Now there are 250 world-wide – nine company and the rest franchised.

The company has built its business on the ideas that cosmetics could be stripped of expensive packaging and hype, that they could be made of naturally-based and biodegradable ingredients and that its products should not be tested on animals.

Anita Roddick, who started the Body Shop, has undertaken 'a serious commitment to protecting the natural world'. In 1986 the shops created an Environmental Projects Department which has embarked on a two-year programme with Friends of the Earth, joined forces with Greenpeace on whaling issues and encouraged its local shops to initiate or join a host of local and world-wide social and environmental undertakings.

5. *Henry Fairfield Osborne*

Fairfield Osborne (1857–1935), American palaeontologist and museum administrator, was an important figure in the development of vertebrate palaeontology and in the movement to make museums interesting and instructive to the layman. A student, and later professor, at Princeton, and Da Costa Professor of Biology (Zoology) at Columbia University, he organized and headed the vertebrate palaeontology department of the American Museum of Natural History, becoming president of the Museum in 1908. He undertook a considerable amount of work for the New York Zoological Society and for other bodies.

Some of his ideas, such as that of adaptive radiation, became fundamental evolutionary theory but his idea of evolution normally proceeding in parallel lines in predetermined directions and his belief that mutation is an accident interfering with, rather than determining the direction of evolution, were generally rejected. He published nearly a thousand books and papers and, more than anyone else, made 'dinosaur' a household word.

III THE POPULATION FACTOR   pp. 135–93

1. ### *The Margaret Pyke Trust*

This British charity, founded in 1969, sets out to provide supplementary services to the clinical ones provided by the National Health Service in the area of family planning. It aims to provide improved methods of contraception, assists in the training of doctors and nurses and raises money for research and education.

In partnership with London's Bloomsbury Health Authority (the statutory NHS body) it runs a medical centre for a broad range of family planning matters, the Trust paying research salaries and for some of the projects.

Margaret Pyke, who had been associated with the family planning movement from 1931, was chairman of the Family Planning Association from 1954 until her death in 1966. Her successor as chairman of the FPA was Lady Medawar, a founder, and now director, of the Trust.

2. ### *Common Ground International*

Common Ground International is an informal grouping of organizations and agencies with overlapping areas of concern (either of problem or solution), thus giving them common ground. In broad outline they work in the fields of population control, wildlife conservation and the safeguarding and development of the environment.

Representatives meet several times a year to discuss current issues and to work out the possibilities for joint programmes of action or pressure. Lady Medawar and the

Margaret Pyke Trust have often co-ordinated the group's activities.

3. *The Conservation for Development Centre*

The Conservation for Development Centre, a non-profit making organization, was established in Gland, at the headquarters of the IUCN in 1981. The unit works to encourage those undertaking development projects to take account of the principles of conservation. It provides expert advice to governments and aid agencies throughout the world. It is currently involved in over 70 projects, most of them in the developing world.

4. *Badgers and Bovine Tuberculosis*

Although some people have expressed doubt about the role of badgers in the spread of bovine TB, scientific opinion generally supported the Ministry of Agriculture's policy of killing badgers in areas of infection, which it was hoped would discourage the indiscriminate killing of badgers by farmers worried for their cattle.

In 1982 the policy of gassing badgers ended and was replaced by cage-trapping of the live animals and shooting in the traps. This avoided some of the uncertainties of gassing and made bodies more easily available for post mortem examination. Until 1986 extermination was carried outwards from an area of infection until none was found, since then it has been limited to farms where cattle have been infected and no action taken until all other possible non-badger sources of infection have been investigated and ruled out. From the end of 1986 badger control has been voluntary, not compulsory – a farmer or land owner can now 'opt out'.

IV THE VICTIMS pp. 195–272

1. *Run-off*

Run-off is the water discharged in surface streams, not only that which flows along the surface, but also all that above the ground-water level which seeps through the surface to reach a stream. As it washes the surface or soaks through the soil it collects some of the chemicals on or in the soil and carries them far from the place where they were originally used, to pollute streams and rivers.

2. *Mersey Bird Death*

These bird deaths were due to organic lead poisoning and the cause went back over a long period. The original source was the production of an anti-knock petrol product by a company which, since the 1950s, has discharged lead products into the Manchester Ship Canal. Although this practice had been stopped long before the disaster, the lead had built up in the canal sediments and in invertebrates in the canal. Then, in 1980, an exceptionally high tide flushed sediments out of the canal into the Mersey, where the lead was absorbed by more invertebrates. The birds were poisoned when they ate these lead-loaded invertebrates.

3. *The 1973 Oil Crisis*

This oil crisis, one result of the 1973 Arab-Israeli War, left the developed world feeling shaken and vulnerable. When, in October 1973, Israel occupied Egyptian territories, the Arab oil producers of the Organization of Petroleum Exporting Countries (OPEC) showed their dissatisfaction with countries they believed to be friendly to Israel by restricting oil supplies to Europe and Japan and withholding them entirely from the USA and the Netherlands (the latter country because Royal Dutch Shell was part owner of the Basrah Petroleum Company, which the Arabs then nationalized). By March 1974 the embargoes were lifted and full supplies restored.

INDEX

Fontana Paperbacks: Non-fiction

Fontana is a leading paperback publisher of non-fiction, both popular and academic.

- ☐ Street Fighting Years *Tariq Ali* £3.95
- ☐ The Boys and the Butterflies *James Birdsall* £3.95
- ☐ Time and Chance *James Callaghan* £5.95
- ☐ Jane Fonda *Michael Freedland* £3.95
- ☐ Perestroika *Mikhail Gorbachev* £3.95
- ☐ The Real Charles *Alan Hamilton* £3.95
- ☐ Going For It! *Victor Kiam* £3.95
- ☐ Keep Going For It! *Victor Kiam* £3.95
- ☐ In the Name of the Working Class *Sandor Kopacsi* £3.95
- ☐ Lucan: Not Guilty *Sally Moore* £3.95
- ☐ Yamani *Jeffrey Robinson* £3.95
- ☐ Don't Ask the Price *Marcus Sieff* £3.95
- ☐ Nor Iron Bars a Cage *Penelope Tremayne* £3.95
- ☐ Just Williams *Kenneth Williams* £2.95

You can buy Fontana paperbacks at your local bookshop or newsagent. Or you can order them from Fontana Paperbacks, Cash Sales Department, Box 29, Douglas, Isle of Man. Please send a cheque, postal or money order (not currency) worth the purchase price plus 22p per book for postage (maximum postage required is £3).

NAME (Block letters) _____

ADDRESS _____

_____

_____

While every effort is made to keep prices low, it is sometimes necessary to increase them at short notice. Fontana Paperbacks reserve the right to show new retail prices on covers which may differ from those previously advertised in the text or elsewhere.